Ablaze

Ablaze

Igniting Spiritual Passion for Life
Through Reading God's Word

PAM GILLASPIE

GREEN KEY BOOKS
Holiday, Florida

Table of Contents

With love for Brad, Katie, and Dave
Follow Him with your whole hearts!

For the eyes of the LORD *move to and fro throughout the earth*
that He may strongly support those whose heart is completely His.
II Chronicles 16:9a

Foreword

IT IS SOMETHING MOST OF US WANT. It is something most of us don't know how to get. It scares us, it overwhelms us, and it makes us shy away. What is "It"? It is passion—a holy passion for God. It sounds exciting, but it sounds like something only people with no hormones and no past might be able to achieve. It is desirable but, oh, so unattainable. That would be what one would think, but Pam Gillaspie has debunked every lie that has blocked regular people like you and me from going after a passionate relationship with God.

With great wisdom and down to earth practicality, Pam calls out and says, "This is not rocket science!" What a comforting word. It is not as hard as you might think. It is easier than you dreamed, and it is available to anyone who really wants to have it. A holy passion for God comes out of a determined, purposeful relationship with His Word. He has said what He has to say. He has invited us to know Him, and yet many of us, who call ourselves Christians, don't know who He is or what He is like. We wonder, we guess, and we rely on our pastors and priests to fill us in on what they think but a very small percentage of us really know.

If you want a relationship with God that takes you beyond a nodding acquaintance, this very direct and easy-to-read book is for you. Pam is innovative, creative and very pragmatic. Any one can take her directions and become God-seekers and God-knowers. There is no fog. There is no spiritual smoke. There is no "let me impress you with the big words I know." With humility but great intelligence, Pam puts the Word of God at your fingertips. She makes it easy, down to how to find a Bible that fits your lifestyle.

Pam is passionate. If you read *Ablaze*, you cannot avoid being ignited with holy passion. I love it and recommend it without reservation.

Jan Silvious
Chattanooga, Tennessee

Preface

FOR WHATEVER REASON, God has put in me a burning passion for His Word. I know that it is not of my own doing, and I know that it is to accomplish His purposes.

However, I need to confess from the start my feelings of inadequacy in writing a book of this nature, a book on spiritual passion, because I know that I have so much yet to learn. There is still much of "me" that needs to be consumed by Jesus. I don't know about you, but whenever I encounter an author or speaker who has not been "around the block" a couple of times, so to speak, I listen with a more critical ear than I do with someone more, shall we say, chronologically seasoned.

I often feel as though I can't address a topic because I don't know everything there is to know...as though I someday will. So, with that said, I hope you will read this book with the understanding that it is not written by a person who in any way claims to "know it all." I pray you will weigh and measure absolutely everything I say against the Word of God, and if any of my ideas come up lacking, toss them. I believe my God-given calling in life is to point people to the Word of God and the God of the Word. This book is nothing more than a tool to point you to His Book.

Pam Gillaspie

Introduction

I AM AMAZED AT HOW MANY PEOPLE, particularly churched people, are looking for spiritual passion but overlook the Bible. It boggles my mind. We are a culture that looks so strongly to feelings and experiences that often those feelings and experiences become an end in themselves. We go to church and hang out around the Word of God, hoping that something "spiritual" will rub off on us.

It is closely akin to the person who thinks he can contract a blood-borne disease by sitting in the same room with contaminated blood. Nothing is going to happen unless there is contact. Sure, there are plenty of diseases out there to catch, so much so that over the years we have changed the way we do medicine.

Think about it. Back when I was in high school working as a dental assistant, we gave the dental tools a good scrubbing in hot water. Today, we are throwing the stuff away because of the danger of contamination. Medical and dental professionals wear gloves and goggles to keep from coming in contact with potential contaminants. We all know that the way one contracts a communicable disease is by coming in contact with it.

Oddly enough, spiritual passion is caught in much the same way. The primary means God uses for igniting spiritual passion in His people is contact with His Word. You can sit *by* your Bible, you can read *about* your Bible, you can read all the Christian self-help books on the shelves, you can listen to good sermons and rock to great Christian tunes, and you can hang out in Christendom for a lifetime without being genuinely infected. You want a serious "case" of Jesus? Open the Book.

SPIRITUAL HOT ZONES

A few years back, I read a best-selling non-fiction book that scared me about as bad as any horror novel you could read. It was called *The Hot Zone*. Ever read it? It is a story about the Ebola virus. I'm sure you're probably familiar with that. It's a deadly virus that lives in Africa near Lake Victoria. It kills in a very ugly way and very, very quickly.

The book actually documents a strain of Ebola that ended up in Reston, Virginia, in lab chimpanzees. There was very real concern about it causing a medical mess the likes of which we could probably not even imagine. Obviously, the situation in Virginia was resolved, but the book marked me because of the picture it painted of hot zones.

The name of the book comes from science. When scientists and others deal with contagions that are this dangerous, they deal with them in hot zones. A hot zone is a place of intense concentration of a contagious agent. We're talking about suits with layers of gloving, bleach decontamination chambers on exit, special enclosed ventilation systems, the whole works because of the dangers involved.

So the deal is that in order to catch a contagious disease, you need to come in contact with it. Wear the gloves, wear the goggles, rinse in bleach, and you'll come away from the most highly contagious agent unaffected.

Friends, it is time for the church to take off the spiritual gloves and goggles and let the Word of God wash over us. It is time to "catch" some passion by being in the hot zone of the Word of God.

You know, though, passion for Christ and His Word is not an end in itself. Sometimes it seems that the selfishness we are taught in our culture pervades to the very depths of our souls. We want Jesus for ourselves, for the comfort He brings without the burden of bringing Him to others. We want Jesus as an end in Himself. Please read closely here and don't misunderstand. Jesus *is* the end in Himself. He is the Alpha and Omega, the beginning and the end. He is ultimately all we will ever want or need. *But*, and this is a big one, He did not leave us on earth just to enjoy Him and to keep Him to ourselves. When Jesus left, He sent us on a mission. We are to take His Word to the entire world and to make disciples.

BECOMING A SPIRITUAL HOT ZONE

So as we go forward on our journey together, we will look first at practical ways we can increase our contact with the Word of God so that we can become infected—set ablaze with holy passion. As we come into contact with the Word, we will see God transforming us into people of the Word, people of passion who love their God and love others and are on His mission to take His Word to the ends of the earth.

Now I know, what you're thinking. "Come on, Pam, people just can't get that set on fire by the Bible. Like, I'm going to read the Bible and become passionate and 'infectious' myself. I'm just not buying what you're selling."

I understand the objection because when you look around the church today people who are crazy about the Word of God are not exactly the overwhelming majority. And others who profess to love the Word are betrayed by their actions that show they only love the knowledge it brings. They have handled it up close, but they have handled it gloved, and it has never really infected the heart. If it is all about the head and not about the obedience of faith, knowledge of the Word can puff us up and fail to transform us. I hate to say that, but it is reality.

I understand the objection. I have an academic background in Bible study and have read liberal scholars who know all about the Bible, but who have never met Jesus.

The fact, though, that some handle the Word gloved and remain unchanged does not negate the inherent power in the Word of God. In fact, those who have been truly transformed, who are truly people of the Word, shine out and are very hard to miss on the landscape of life.

Maybe it is because of the darkness in the church and the world that those who are spiritually passionate shine like beacons. I will never forget the passion that many of my college professors had as they spoke of Jesus and all things theological. Although my head and heart were still pretty far apart back in those days, I saw something very real in those men...something that I wanted as reality in my life. They were carriers of something I desperately wanted. Maybe I'm just weird, but when I see a life coming more and more into conformity with the Word of God, my soul shouts out, "God, make me like that!"

I just can't help but think that His response to that request would be, "Child, draw near and read my words!"

Part 1

Drawing Near
the Flame

The Power of the Word

—1—

Any Old Bush Will Burn

THE TRANSFORMING POWER THAT GOD UNLEASHES through His Word literally changes lives. We know this, don't we? We read from time to time about people in the Bible who were simply over the top for God. We see the neighbor down the street who is fired up for Jesus not just in the way she talks, but also in the nitty-gritty of life. We go to a conference and hear that special speaker who has spiritual passion radiating a twelve foot circle around her. We see our pastor tirelessly laboring for the Gospel of Christ because of his overwhelming love for the Savior and for His people. We have this friend who actually has purpose in life and seems to know truth. We see people who have been set ablaze by God, and in them, we catch glimpses of what our lives might be if God set us ablaze with a holy passion for Himself.

Why is it that the life-changing power of the Word of God is always changing some other person's life? I think it is very often because the enemy is selling lies, and we are snatching them up like sale shoes at Nine West. Perhaps we fail once in our reading, we find something we don't understand, we have a hard time sticking with Bible reading, and all of a sudden we find ourselves believing that we can't study the Bible. It's too hard. We will just never understand it. But these are lies...all of them! The truth is, as the old saying goes, "any old bush will burn" when it is set ablaze by God.

As we look at how to draw near to God through His Word, I am going to offer some very practical suggestions. You see, I've failed in almost every possible way in Bible reading, which makes me something of an expert in the area of what not to do.

Remember, the goal we have is getting into God's Word and falling more and more in love with Him and His Word. Every suggestion I make, every suggested reading or assignment has that in mind. Everything in this book is designed to help you get into the Word of God. If you start reading this book and halfway through find yourself bored with me and enthralled with God's Word, then please, pass this book along to someone else and marinate in the true Word!

GETTING STARTED

Don't become depressed if you're not that far along on this journey. If you're not that far along, you're not that far along. It's all right. Just ask God to help you. Remember, no one comes to God as a spiritual adult.

Let's think about our spiritual journey as if it were a physical trip from Chicago to Florida like the one my family does on an almost annual basis. Many of us don't have the patience for a long car ride through Marion, Illinois, to Paducah, Kentucky, on to Nashville and Chattanooga and Atlanta, and finally to the Sunshine State. We want a jet to pick us up in front of our house and sweep us to Florida in a couple of hours. Spiritual growth, however, doesn't happen that fast. It takes time. In fact, it looks more like an extended car trip than a ride on a jet.

So whether you're all the way to Atlanta, spiritually speaking, or just getting out of the Chicago suburbs, remember that a trip takes time. The only way you get where you're going is by getting started in the first place.

And speaking of getting started, at the end of each chapter, you're going to find a section entitled, "Drawing Near." Here you will find opportunities to get into the Word of God for yourself in ways that, hopefully, will spur you on to more and more and more and more reading. However, before you look at all of the opportunities for reading, and keel over in sheer excitement, you need to know that you are not supposed to take advantage of all of them. At least not all at once. I am often grieved by people who decide not to study God's Word at all because they feel that if they become part of a Bible study group, for instance, they may not be able to finish everything the class requires; they may not be able to do it just the way they'd like. That has got to be on Satan's top ten list of effective lies. This study doesn't have a bottom line amount of homework to be completed each week. It is purposely designed to ebb and flow with your life and to push you more and more to read, not just this book, but God's Book.

In Part 1, I'm going to offer some gut-level practical suggestions for reading God's Word, many of which I've learned from the experience of trying approaches that haven't worked. I'm all for learning from other people's mistakes, and in this section you'll have the opportunity to learn from some of mine without having to learn by making the same mistakes yourself.

If the operative words of Part 1 are "How To," then the operative words of Part 2 are "So What?" So we've learned to read the Bible, so we've drawn near to the flame, what then should our lives look like?

Part 1 is all about drawing near to the flame of God's Word while Part 2 looks at being set ablaze by God and His Word and considers the mission to which Christ has called us.

With that said, you should understand that my goal is not to present a system, per se. Rather it is to help you identify barriers to reading. To help you identify lies you've snapped up and wrong thinking patterns that you probably haven't even considered to be faulty. It is to help you to remove them so you can put yourself more and more into contact with God's life-changing Word—to draw near the flame.

GETTING UNSTUCK

So often our minds simply get "stuck in the mud," and we find that we are crippling ourselves by limiting our thinking. For instance, we let the enemy tell us that we can't read the Bible, and we just take him at his word.

My mind goes to the story of the woman who always cut the end off the roast before putting it in the oven. One day as she was preparing dinner for the family, her daughter asked her, "Mommy, why do you always cut the end off of the roast before you cook it?" Her mom answered, "Well, sweetie, that's what Grandma always did." The girl was not satisfied. Later that evening, when the extended family arrived for dinner, the girl asked her grandma, "Grandma, why did you always cut the end off the roast before cooking it?" Grandma answered, looking over at her mother, the girl's great grandmother, "I always did it, because that's how Great-Granny always prepared her roasts." The girl looked toward Great-Granny, who laughed and said, "I cut off the end of the roast because it wouldn't fit in the pan."

For years, I kept "cutting the end off the roast" in my Bible reading. I had developed set ways of thinking that I constantly applied to my Bible reading, thoughts like:

+ If I'm going to read through the Bible, then I need to start at the beginning and read through to the end.

+ If I'm going to read the Bible, then I have to understand everything that I read right away.

+ If I'm going to read the Bible, then I have to have "quiet" time and read under perfect conditions.

+ If I'm going to read through the Bible, then I have to stick to a set reading schedule.

+ If I'm going to read through the Bible, then I have to muster up the energy to do it by myself—and I just can't. I simply don't have it in me.

I don't know exactly when I picked up these thoughts, but I operated by them, nonetheless, and each in its own way hampered me as I sought to read. They became real barriers to reading through my Bible. Every time I tried to read, I went about it the same way, with the same set of presuppositions, listening to the same lies from the enemy, and every time with the same results...failure. I got stuck. I wanted to read the entire counsel of the Word of God. Honestly, I did, but I felt powerless to accomplish the task. Finally, I started praying that God would give me a relentless desire for His Word. And that is where it all begins, asking God for the desire. As He answered that prayer, and as I began reading, God helped me out of the ruts I had been in and revolutionized my reading.

As you read, feel free to skim over the truths. You may already have a handle on some of truths we'll talk about, so don't linger there. Spend your time in the areas where you need help. Don't waste time on issues that don't apply to your situation. Don't waste time on my words unless they will help point you to His Words. The goal here is not for you to get a heapin' helpin' of my opinions, but to help you get into the very Word of God itself. His Words, ultimately, are the only words that matter.

Calling the Man

In my family and extended family, we have a phrase that gets bantered about quite often. "Call the man." You see, "call the man" is what you do when the man (or woman) of the house can't deal with a problem at hand either because of a lack of ability, skill, knowledge, or time. The toilet's plugged up and no amount of plunging seems to work. "Call the man." The freezer sounds like a raccoon is dying somewhere in its bowels. "Call the man." Something smokes every time the dryer is started. "Call the man."

Have you had a "call the man" incident in your household recently? Most of us do from time to time. But sometimes, for whatever reason, we don't "call the man." Instead, we sort meander along with the problem hanging around. We kind of ignore it and hope it will go away or that someone else will deal with it.

We had one of those not too long ago. It was a bitter cold Chicago night and for some reason, my house was full of children…and dogs. Ten, as I recall—seven human, three canine. I was minding my own business in another room of the house and trying to put some distance between the pack and myself when I noticed a child slinking past his father and into the room where I was. When big things break, most children seem to prefer Mom. As my then fourth-grader approached, I could almost hear the ka-ching of repair bills in my head. The victim: a double-paned thermal window in the corner of the living room had been assaulted by a posse of kids and dogs all piling onto one badly placed recliner. What happened wasn't a pretty sight.

My husband patched the inner pane with duct tape—the universal repair tool—and we ignored the broken window for a while. After all, it was sub-zero outside. It was the middle of the winter, and we didn't want to take the window out and then take it somewhere leaving us exposed to the elements. We also figured that if we "called the man," he'd probably have to take it with him too, it would cost even more, and we'd still be without a window for some time. So we decided to wait until warmer weather. We knew there was nothing we could do in our own power to fix it apart from "calling the man" or bringing the window to "the man."

Well, warmer weather came and went, and it came and went again. I kept waiting for someone to take the window out and take it to "the man." It obviously wasn't fixing itself. It was, after all, hidden in a corner and, oh, so fashionably taped. One day, I finally had had enough. I picked up the phone and "called the man." What happened amazed me. A couple of days later "the man" came and measured my window. He told me how much a replacement would cost. I learned that this type of window couldn't be fixed. It has to be replaced. He ordered the new window and put it in a few days later. Sure, the one hundred fifty bucks set me back a bit, but I had no other options. I can't fix a window. The only way for me to confront this problem was to call for help.

It is exactly the same thing when it comes to reading your Bible. It's not something you can pull off on your own. Please understand that I mean absolutely no irreverence here. I am simply making an analogy: When it comes to drawing near to God through His Word, we need to "call the Man" in prayer. Oh, how He longs to answer the prayers of those who long to know Him better!

Take a moment to read some of Jesus' last words to His disciples before He went to the cross. They are recorded in the gospel of John in chapters fifteen through seventeen printed below.

As you read these three chapters, take a pen or pencil and mark any reference(s) you can find in which Jesus tells His disciples to pray or to ask things of the Father.

JOHN 15

I am the true vine, and My Father is the vinedresser. Every branch in Me that does not bear fruit, He takes away; and every [branch] that bears fruit, He prunes it so that it may bear more fruit. You are already clean because of the word which I have spoken to you. Abide in Me, and I in you. As the branch cannot bear fruit of itself unless it abides in the vine, so neither [can] you unless you abide in Me. I am the vine, you are the branches; he who abides in Me and I in him, he bears much fruit, for apart from Me you can do nothing. If anyone does not abide in Me, he is thrown away as a branch and dries up; and they gather them, and cast them into the fire and they are burned. If you abide in Me, and My words abide in you, ask whatever you wish, and it will be done for you. My Father is glorified by this, that you bear much fruit, and [so] prove to be My disciples. Just as the Father has loved Me, I have also loved you; abide in My love. If you keep My commandments, you will abide in My love; just as I have kept My Father's command-ments and abide in His love. These things I have spoken to you so that My joy may be in you, and [that] your joy may be made full.

This is My commandment, that you love one another, just as I have loved you. Greater love has no one than this, that one lay down his life for his friends. You are My friends if you do what I command you. No longer do I call you slaves, for the slave does not know what his master is doing; but I have called you friends, for all things that I have heard from My Father I have made known to you. You did not choose Me but I chose you, and appointed you that you would go and bear fruit, and [that] your fruit would remain, so that whatever you ask of the Father in My name He may give to you. This I command you, that you love one another.

If the world hates you, you know that it has hated Me before [it hated] you. If you were of the world, the world would love its own; but because you are not of the world, but I chose you out of the world, because of this the world hates you. Remember the word that I said to you, "A slave is not greater than his master." If they persecuted Me, they will also persecute you; if they kept My word, they will keep yours also. But all these things they will do to you for My name's sake, because they do not know the One who sent Me. If I had not come and spoken to them, they would not have sin, but now they have no excuse for their sin. He who hates Me hates My Father also. If I had not done among them the works which no one else did, they would not have sin; but now they have both seen and hated Me and My Father as well. But [they have done this] to fulfill the word that is written in their Law, "They hated Me without a cause."

When the Helper comes, whom I will send to you from the Father, [that is] the Spirit of truth who proceeds from the Father, He will testify about Me, and you [will] testify also, because you have been with Me from the beginning.

JOHN 16

"These things I have spoken to you so that you may be kept from stumbling. They will make you outcasts from the synagogue, but an hour is coming for everyone who kills you to think that he is offering service to God. These things they will do because they have not known the Father or Me. But these things I have spoken to you, so that when their hour

16

comes, you may remember that I told you of them. These things I did not say to you at the beginning, because I was with you.

"But now I am going to Him who sent Me; and none of you asks Me, 'Where are You going?' But because I have said these things to you, sorrow has filled your heart. But I tell you the truth, it is to your advantage that I go away; for if I do not go away, the Helper will not come to you; but if I go, I will send Him to you. And He, when He comes, will convict the world concerning sin and righteousness and judgment; concerning sin, because they do not believe in Me; and concerning righteousness, because I go to the Father and you no longer see Me; and concerning judgment, because the ruler of this world has been judged.

"I have many more things to say to you, but you cannot bear [them] now. But when He, the Spirit of truth, comes, He will guide you into all the truth; for He will not speak on His own initiative, but whatever He hears, He will speak; and He will disclose [it] to you. He will glorify Me, for He will take of Mine and will disclose to you what is to come. All things that the Father has are Mine; therefore I said that He takes of Mine and will disclose it to you.

"A little while, and you will no longer see Me; and again a little while, and you will see Me." [Some] of His disciples then said to one another, "What is this thing He is telling us, 'A little while, and you will not see Me; and again a little while, and you will see Me'; and, 'because I go to the Father'?" So they were saying, "What is this that He says, 'A little while'? We do not know what He is talking about." Jesus knew that they wished to question Him, and He said to them, "Are you deliberating together about this, that I said, 'A little while, and you will not see Me, and again a little while, and you will see Me'? Truly, truly, I say to you, that you will weep and lament, but the world will rejoice; you will grieve, but your grief will be turned into joy. Whenever a woman is in labor she has pain, because her hour has come; but when she gives birth to the child, she no longer remembers the anguish because of the joy that a child has been born into the world. Therefore you too have grief now; but I will see you again, and your heart will rejoice, and no one [will] take your joy away from you. In that day you will not question Me about anything. Truly, truly, I say to you, if you ask the Father for anything in My name, He will give it to you. Until now you have asked for nothing in My name; ask and you will receive, so that your joy may be made full.

"These things I have spoken to you in figurative language; an hour is coming when I will no longer speak to you in figurative language, but will tell you plainly of the Father. In that day you will ask in My name, and I do not say to you that I will request of the Father on your behalf; for the Father Himself loves you, because you have loved Me and have believed that I came forth from the Father. I came forth from the Father and have come into the world; I am leaving the world again and going to the Father."

His disciples said, "Lo, now You are speaking plainly and are not using a figure of speech. Now we know that You know all things, and have no need for anyone to question You; by this we believe that You came from God." Jesus answered them, "Do you now believe? Behold, an hour is coming, and has [already] come, for you to be scattered, each to his own [home], and to leave Me alone; and [yet] I am not alone, because the Father is with Me. These things I have spoken to you, so that in Me you may have peace. In the world you have tribulation, but take courage; I have overcome the world."

JOHN 17

Jesus spoke these things; and lifting up His eyes to heaven, He said, "Father, the hour has come; glorify Your Son, that the Son may glorify You, even as You gave Him authority over all flesh, that to all whom You have given Him, He may give eternal life. This is eternal life, that they may know You, the only true God, and Jesus Christ whom You have sent. I glorified You on the earth, having accomplished the work *which You have given Me to do. Now, Father, glorify Me together with Yourself, with the glory which I had with You before the world was.*

"I have manifested Your name to the men whom You gave Me out of the world; they were Yours and You gave them to Me, and they have kept Your word. Now they have come to know that everything You have given Me is from You; for the words which You gave Me I have given to them; and they received [them] and truly understood that I came forth from You, and they believed that You sent Me.

"I ask on their behalf; I do not ask on behalf of the world, but of those whom You have given Me; for they are Yours; and all things that are Mine are Yours, and Yours are Mine; and I have been glorified in them. I am no longer in the world; and [yet] they themselves are in the world, and I come to You, Holy Father, keep them in Your name, [the name] which You have given Me, that they may be one even as We [are]. While I was with them, I was keeping them in Your name which You have given Me; and I guarded them and not one of them perished but the son of perdition, so that the Scripture would be fulfilled. But now I come to You; and these things I speak in the world so that they may have My joy made full in themselves. I have given them Your word; and the world has hated them, because they are not of the world, even as I am not of the world. I do not ask You to take them out of the world, but to keep them from the evil [one]. They are not of the world, even as I am not of the world. Sanctify them in the truth; Your word is truth. As You sent Me into the world, I also have sent them into the world. For their sakes I sanctify Myself, that they themselves also may be sanctified in truth.

"I do not ask on behalf of these alone, but for those also who be-lieve in Me through their word; that they may all be one; even as You, Father, [are] in Me and I in You, that they also may be in Us, so that the world may believe that You sent Me. The glory which You have giv-en Me I have given to them, that they may be one, just as We are one; I in them and You in Me, that they may be perfected in unity, so that the

world may know that You sent Me, and loved them, even as You have loved Me. Father, I desire that they also, whom You have given Me, be with Me where I am, so that they may see My glory which You have given Me, for You loved Me before the foundation of the world.

"O righteous Father, although the world has not known You, yet I have known You; and these have known that You sent Me; and I have made Your name known to them, and will make it known, so that the love with which You loved Me may be in them, and I in them."

Questions

1. What did Jesus say about making requests of God?
2. What did Jesus have to say about the Holy Spirit?
3. What role do you see prayer and the Holy Spirit playing in your life?

When we come to God humbly in prayer, there is a sense in which we are taking off the rubber gloves of our soul. We are opening ourselves up to "catch" what He's giving. It is His work, but we are no longer in a state of resisting, or as Paul would put it in the book of Romans, of holding down the truth. As you prepare today to draw near to God through His Word, ask Him to help you to remember to seek Him in prayer every time you open your Bible.

Drawing Near

As you go along throughout your week, pick one—or several—of the opportunities for drawing near. Some days you'll have more time than usual. Other days you'll be so busy and stressed that you'll find drawing near to God to be your only refuge. Some days you'll have running noses running around the house or other metaphorical fires to put out, and you may not be able to draw near to God through His Word as much as you'd like.

Would you do something for me? Would you consider resolving right now that this will be okay? Decide that you won't go overboard and take the attitude, "If I can't do as much as I think I should, I'm not going to do anything at all." One of the favorite sayings that my Precept class has is, "Some is better than none." So, now's your chance. Ask God to guide you with His Spirit—and let's begin learning to draw near to the fire by completing one or a few of the following:

- Review the high priestly prayer of Jesus in John 15–17 and commit to memory one or several key verses on prayer.
- Read the apostle John's other letters: 1 John, 2 John, and 3 John.
- Read the full gospel of John.
- Read the Sermon on the Mount located in Matthew 5–7 to see what else Jesus has to say about making requests of the Father. Note what you learned.

FIVE LIBERATING TRUTHS FOR READING YOUR BIBLE

—2—

The Truth About Order

You Don't Have to Start in Genesis

HOW MANY PEOPLE DO YOU KNOW who have read Genesis and Exodus more times than they can remember? Maybe you are one of them. I certainly am. For some reason, we in the western culture have this thing about picking up a book, starting on the first page, and going straight on through to the end. Not that there's anything wrong with that, particularly if you are reading fiction; it just isn't necessary when you are reading the Bible, a book that is actually a compilation of various shorter writings. Chances are you already realize from at least one failure that reading from the start of the Bible and trying to go straight through poses an enormous challenge.

Sure, it's the same amount of material regardless of the order in which you read. But, practically speaking, your odds of actually finishing Leviticus and Numbers increase dramatically if you don't try to tackle them in order.

Unlike most books that are arranged strictly chronologically, the Bible has been compiled by general categories. Sure, it starts with the creation of the world and ends with the new heaven and new earth with Christ as the ultimate Victor. This certainly gives the casual observer the sense of chronology, but in between, the books are generally clumped together more by genre than chronology. We see the Old Testament falling into the general categories of Law, History, Poetry, and Prophecy, and in the New Testament we see mainly Gospels, Epistles (letters), and Prophecy.

So why does reading from the beginning pose such a problem for so many of us? Basically, because it sets people up for failure, and failure leads to resignation. We all start off with excitement, thinking we can read straight through the Bible. We try hard. Sometimes we try hard over and over. We fail. We give up. We end up with a scenario that goes something like this:

+ I am going to read through the Bible this year. I know I can do it. I'm starting in Genesis and by next December, I'll be finishing up Revelation.

+ I can't believe how long Leviticus is. I will never be able to get through this book, much less the entire Bible. I really thought it would be different this time. But I've tried and failed so often, I'll bet I just don't have it in me to do it.

+ You know, I'd love to read through the entire Bible, but I've tried and failed so many times that I just don't believe I can do it. I'll stick to devotionals. They're more on my level. The pastor will teach me what I need to know. I'm just not smart enough or disciplined enough or whatever...I just can't do it!

Satan loves it when we think, for whatever reason, that we can't read our Bibles. Separated from the Word, we are impotent for the kingdom of God. And unfortunately, that is exactly where many people who call themselves Christians are today. We have failed at reading the Bible, so we believe that we don't have the skills to handle the Bible at all. That is a lie!

The truth of the matter is this: You don't have to read the Bible in order! I know, you may not believe me, but it's true! To help you get started in reading "out of order," here are a few practical tips I've picked up along the way.

1. Try starting with 1 Samuel.

If you've been a Christian for any length of time at all, chances are pretty good that you have had at least a measure of success in reading some New Testament books. It's the Old Testament that seems like the highest mountain to scale. After all, it's about three times as long as the New Testament. It has books like Leviticus and Ezekiel and Job. The longest chapter in the Old Testament (Psalm 119) is longer than several of the New Testament books! So, in my estimation, any attempt at reading through the Bible needs to start with a successful dip into the Old Testament. To be perfectly honest, I tend to be a person who likes to get the hardest stuff out of the way first so I can cruise home with material that's a little easier, but I don't recommend that approach with the Old Testament.

In reading the Old Testament, I've found 1 Samuel a wonderful place to start. It reads like a story and is not nearly as long as the books of the Law. Beginning with the story of Hannah, the mother of the prophet Samuel as she cries out to God for a son, the book of 1 Samuel also tells the story of Saul, the first King of Israel, of David and Goliath, and of the continual pursuit of David by Saul. It concludes with the death of Saul, setting the reader up for a continued trip into 2 Samuel. This narrative, then, continues right into 1 and 2 Kings.

At the end of 2 Kings, the people of Israel went into captivity, which led me in my reading to the books of Jeremiah and Lamentations that have to do with the Babylonian captivity.

2. Remember that the Old Testament is filled with stories.

Indulge me here for one more quick point on the Old Testament in general. Have you picked up a children's Bible anytime recently? If so, what have you seen? That's right, a heavy helping of stories from the Old Testament. Sure, you'll find stories about Jesus, too, and a few about Paul. But you'll have tons of Old Testament stories! I don't use the word story here in the sense of something fictitious, but to help you connect with the fact that much of the Old Testament is captivating reading. When brought to the appropriate developmental level, it holds the attention of kids—and they can be some of the toughest critics out there! It is also understandable to kids, which means you can get it too!

3. Even if you're tempted, don't start in Genesis.

Another day, another time…try it then. Try starting in Genesis when you have already successfully made your way through the entire Bible more than once. Don't get me wrong, Genesis is great reading, it is just so toward the front of the book, and it is so long (fifty chapters). The problem is that you'll be reading for a long time before you really sense that you are making progress. If you start further in, you'll feel like you're making progress faster and be more inclined to keep going. The other problem with starting in Genesis is that even if you do make it through this book in a relatively timely fashion, you'll be tempted to continue on in a linear fashion and will soon find out how hard it is to read the end of Exodus, all of Leviticus, and the beginning of Numbers consecutively. And even if you do make it through those and cruise on toward the "easy-reading" historical books, you will eventually hit the wall known as Isaiahjeremiahlamentationsezekiel.

Sure, Lamentations is only five chapters long, but have you done a page count on the other three lately? They're good when they're taken in portions, but try to swallow them whole and you'll choke. At least I still do. Maybe the "giants" can ingest these in succession, but for the rest of us, I suggest smaller portions.

One exception here: If you do not have any background in the stories of the Bible from Sunday school experiences or other teaching and do not know the basic stories of Creation, Noah, Abraham, Isaac, Jacob, and Joseph, then you need to start in Genesis. Don't continue in order after that, but do read Genesis first. After that, you might want to try 1 Samuel or one of the Gospels (Matthew, Mark, Luke, or John).

4. Don't think you can ignore the Old Testament.

If you've been a Christian for a while and have never read the Old Testament, you may have reasoned to yourself that because we have a new covenant in Jesus Christ, we really don't need to read what was in the old covenant. As rationalizations go, it sounds pretty good. Given a choice between the two, certainly, you'd have to go with the New Testament. The thing is, though, we can never ever get a grasp on how great the new covenant is without first understanding the old covenant. Much of the New Testament will remain a closed book to you because you won't understand the foundations and you won't have a full understanding of God.

I run into students all the time who get frustrated reading their New Testaments largely, I believe, because they don't have the Old Testament foundation on which the New Testament covenants rest. God gave us the entire Bible for a reason; we need to be about the business of reading all of it.

Not only that, the New Testament tells us that the Old Testament provides us examples, both good and bad, about how we should live. In the first letter to the Corinthians, the apostle Paul says in chapter ten verse six, "Now these things happened as examples for us, so that we would not crave evil things as they also craved." He goes on in verses eleven and twelve to say, "Now these things happened to them as an example, and they were written for our instruction, those upon whom the ends of the ages have come. Therefore let him who thinks he stands take heed that he does not fall."

5. Make good use of your table of contents.

Complex Scripture reading systems work for some people. I recently talked to a woman in a Scripture reading program with daily readings from both the Old and New Testaments. She loves it, and it has helped guide her through the Bible. Great!

For most of us, though, the more complex the system, the less chance we'll make it because of the "I missed a day" principle if nothing else. Ever notice how hard it is to catch up when you miss a day on a schedule...any schedule? If the washing machine doesn't run when it's supposed to or the dishes slide by for one meal without being dealt with, the resulting problem is more than the sum of its parts.

Same thing when you're dealing with a strict Bible reading schedule. When you miss a day, the tendency is to want to do the catch up every time. Instead of "having" to read three chapters in a day, all of a sudden you could be looking at six, nine, twelve, or more. Then we have the guilt of looking at what we haven't done. "I should be there by now, but I'm only here."

In my estimation, complex schedules move us squarely into the academic realm. When my eyes see the word "schedule," my soul sees the word "syllabus," and the relational aspect of the activity diminishes.

6. Use mind games to your benefit.

Success tends to breed more success, and failure tends to breed more failure. Discipline breeds discipline, indulgence breeds indulgence. We all know this from just living our lives and watching the lives of others. Take school, for example. Scoring well on a test tends to buoy up a student and spur him or her on to greater things. Once you've achieved ninety-eight percent on a test, you know you've got the right stuff and can pull it off again. The second, third, and fourth times are always easier, because you have the confidence to succeed. Likewise, when you score forty percent after having exerted yourself, it is much harder to gain the courage to try again.

For this reason, it is important to see yourself making progress toward your goal; small successes along the way can help you gain serious momentum. Think with me for a moment about the typical path most people take in reading the Bible, bearing in mind that when you look at the Bible's table of contents you're staring at a list of sixty-six entries. If you start at Genesis and proceed forward, you have ninety chapters in just the first two books. While these books are generally good reading, the check marks for chapters read aren't exactly flying onto the page.

So by the time you hit the Leviticus/Numbers wall, you don't have much in the way of visual "success" to look at in your table of contents. If you have read Genesis and Exodus, you have covered a great deal of ground, but you will likely feel less "on a roll" than if you had knocked off a few of the smaller books first. A "spiritual" way of doing things? Maybe not. But it has worked for me. Remember, we're not looking to be super spiritual here. We are not trying to change ourselves. We're just putting God's Word into our life and letting God do His work from the inside out.

7. Read the epistles in their entirety.

I can't stress this one enough. An epistle is a letter. How do you read a letter? I'm guessing that you do it in one sitting. You don't say, "Okay, I'll read three paragraphs today, three tomorrow, and three on Friday." It just doesn't happen that way, does it? It shouldn't happen that way with epistles either.

So many of us have become five-minute devotional Christians that we really don't know how to sit down and digest a larger portion of Scripture or how to interact and read for more than ten or fifteen minutes at a time. The epistles are a great place to break the "I'll-read-one-chapter-today" habit. Sure, one chapter a day is better than no chapters, but that type of reading can cause problems because we tend to lose context. And it is in context that we understand what the author is really saying. So use the epistles as a training ground for observing context and learning to sit and read for increasing periods of time.

You'll find all of the epistles located in the New Testament. They were letters written to first century churches after Christ had ascended to heaven. Most of them, the Pauline Epistles, were written by the apostle Paul. The name of the book or epistle is taken from the name of the recipients. The Pauline corpus includes the following: Romans, 1 and 2 Corinthians, Galatians, Ephesians, Philippians, Colossians, 1 and 2 Thessalonians, 1 and 2 Timothy, Titus, and Philemon.

The other grouping of epistles you'll find are termed the general epistles. They include: Hebrews, James, 1 and 2 Peter, 1, 2, and 3 John, and Jude. The general epistles generally bear the name of the author as the book title, the epistle to the Hebrews being the exception. Although there is much speculation as to whom the author of Hebrews may be, internal evidence almost certainly rules out the apostle Paul.

8. Read the Minor Prophets in their entirety.
As with the epistles, you're better off reading the Minor Prophets in one sitting. Each prophetic book is relatively short, hence, the term "minor." The minor prophets are Hosea, Joel, Amos, Obadiah, Jonah, Micah, Nahum, Habakkuk, Zephaniah, Haggai, Zechariah, and Malachi. The books range in length from one chapter to fourteen. When reading the prophets, it is essential that you ask, at the very least, these two basic questions to gain a simple understanding of the book:

1. To whom is it written? The answer will usually be Israel (Northern Kingdom) or Judah (Southern Kingdom).
2. When was it written?

The answer you are looking for is before or after the nation has been conquered. Has the nation already been conquered due to judgment or is the book looking forward to and predicting coming judgment?

If you don't have at least a basic understanding of the history of Israel, you'll find it helpful to read some of the historical books in the Bible before moving into the prophets. If, however, you have the basic gist of the divided kingdom and the subsequent captivities, feel free to zip through the minor prophets early on and finish what looks in the table of contents to be about a quarter of the Old Testament.

SIDEBAR HISTORY LESSON
In the Old Testament we hear, among other things, the story of the people of Israel. But sometimes we hear the name Judah thrown in, or references to Jerusalem or Samaria. At first glance, the names can be quite

confusing, but Old Testament history is easier than you'd first think once you start getting a few simple facts under your belt.

FAMILY TREE

The people of Israel take their name from the grandson of Abraham, whom we usually hear referred to as Jacob. God, however, renames him Israel, and from this comes the name of the Jewish people—Israel.

DEFINITIONS:

ISRAEL – The name given to Jacob by God. Later becomes the name of the nation descended from him. Eventually, Israel becomes a divided nation, with two of the twelve tribes remaining with Rehoboam, the son of Solomon, while the other ten tribes follow Jeroboam. These ten tribes retain the name Israel. The capital of Israel was Samaria. It is also referred to as the Northern Kingdom. All of the kings of the North were evil, some more, some less. Israel was captured in 722 BC by Assyria. Most of the inhabitants were deported and scattered; the remaining ones intermarried with other people groups who were brought into Israel by Assyria.

JUDAH – Judah was one of the sons of Jacob (Israel). Judah was originally one of the twelve tribes of Israel. After the division of the kingdom, however, it was used to refer to the two tribes that remained with Rehoboam, the son of Solomon, while the other ten tribes followed Jeroboam. The capital of Judah was Jerusalem. It is also referred to as the Southern Kingdom. In the Southern Kingdom, the kings were a mixed bag of some good, some bad, some very bad. Judah was captured in 586 BC by Babylon. The inhabitants were taken into captivity in Babylon for seventy years and then were allowed to return to their land.

EPHRAIM – While the Northern Kingdom is usually referred to as Israel, it is occasionally called Ephraim. This is not just an attempt to confuse you. Rather, the name is taken from the largest tribe in the Northern Kingdom.

SAMARIA – Samaria was the capital of Israel, the Northern Kingdom of ten tribes that followed non-Davidic kings.

JERUSALEM – Jerusalem was the capital of Judah, the Southern Kingdom of the two tribes that followed the Davidic kings.

UNITED KINGDOM – Israel was a united kingdom of twelve tribes under the leadership first of Saul, and then of David and his son, Solomon.

DIVIDED KINGDOM – Solomon's son, Rehoboam, ticked people off big time—so much so that ten of the tribes took off to follow a man named Jeroboam.

NORTHERN KINGDOM – Ten northern tribes ruled by non-Davidic kings. Also referred to as "Israel." The capital was Samaria.

SOUTHERN KINGDOM – Two southern tribes ruled by the Davidic line of kings. Comprised of the tribes of Judah and Benjamin, the Southern Kingdom is referred to simply as "Judah." The capital of the Southern Kingdom was Jerusalem.

9. Read Hebrews and Leviticus in succession.
I see your eyebrows going up. Leviticus by itself can be a tough read; truth be told, so can Hebrews. However, if you have just finished the book of Hebrews, which focuses on Jesus as our Great High Priest, you will find that Leviticus is very helpful in understanding what is going on in Hebrews and vice versa. All of a sudden, with a reference point of Christ, everything makes a little more sense.

10. Read Leviticus in three sittings tops; try to do it in one sitting.
I had a great childhood. For the most part. I knew without a doubt that my parents loved me, but...they made me eat vegetables. To this day, I can remember the taste of cold beets, feel the squish of cold green beans, and vividly recall the gagging sensation as I tried to swallow them as close to whole as possible with a swig of cold milk. Every day my Dad would

say, "Pam, if you'll just eat them while they're warm, and get it over with, it won't be so bad." And every day, I would dawdle at the dinner table, stretching those veggies out until they practically turned to mold on my plate.

All this to say that for me, reading through Leviticus a chapter a day is like trying to swallow cold vegetables whole. Leviticus is an entire book of do's and don'ts for ancient Israel. (I saw that yawn.) Are there lessons to be learned in Leviticus? Absolutely! Will I see these lessons the first time I read it? Maybe not. Will it be as fun to read as the gospel of John? No. Regardless of what you seem to "get out of it" the first time through, even Leviticus will help you understand the whole context of the Bible. It will help you to see how high and extensive the standards of God are— how impossible it is to be a "law-keeper." It will help you to understand the seriousness of sin and the holiness of God.

Is Leviticus a place to stop and study deeply? Eventually. But on a first trip through the Bible, I would suggest clearing an hour and swallowing whole. This time through, we want to become familiar with the general context of the Bible, the broad sweeping strokes on the canvas, so that when we go back to study in-depth we have a better understanding of the whole. Leviticus is one place that can slow you down; don't let it happen this time.

11. When you're having a hard time reading, stick to the historical books or the Gospels.

Sometimes reading the Bible just gets to be too hard. Maybe you're behind at work, or the kids are super growly, or you'd do anything to just sit and watch TV for a while. Whether it's spiritual warfare or just the circumstances of life, there will be times when opening your Bible is tough. That's when it's the most important to "just do it." You don't want to get into a martyr mode, however. You know what I mean, "Oh, I know that ER is on, but I guess I'll just sit here and read Leviticus instead and see how (sigh) I can apply it to my life today." If you're struggling, try to read for a while in the books that are easier. In general, the historical books and the Gospels tend to read like stories.

The Gospels, Matthew, Mark, Luke, and John, open up the New Testament. The first three, Matthew, Mark, and Luke are often referred to as the synoptic Gospels because they tell the stories of Jesus in a similar fashion and have some overlapping accounts. Why three? Three different audiences. Matthew wrote to a primary Jewish audience, Mark to Romans, and Luke, the physician, wrote to a Greek audience. The gospel of John takes a slightly different approach to the presentation of Jesus, being written around seven major signs Jesus performed with the specific purpose that the readers might "believe that Jesus is the Christ, the Son of God, and believing have life in His name."

12. When you're feeling "behind," rip off a few minor prophets or epistles in a single sitting.
I realize this may sound unspiritual, but realize we don't have to be in a super spiritual mood for God to work in our hearts and our minds. Sometimes we just need that mental boost of checking off a few books. And with twelve minor prophets ranging in length from one chapter (Obadiah) to fourteen (Hosea and Zechariah), the Minor Prophets are a place you can feel like you're really making some progress.

As I mentioned earlier, though, don't dive into these books without first reading some of the historical books unless you have a reasonable understanding of the history of Israel.

13. Hit the major prophets (Isaiah, Jeremiah, Ezekiel), Leviticus, and Numbers when you are "on a roll," but make sure you knock off at least one major prophet relatively early in the your reading.
Some of you may have been stopped by the fact that I didn't include Daniel when I referred to the Major Prophets. While Daniel is usually lumped in with the majors, it is, in fact, a much shorter book and immanently more readable. You could easily park yourself and polish it off in one

enjoyable sitting. The big three, on the other hand, are all in the fifty chapter range, and although there's much great stuff packed in them, the prophets tend to be tougher to grasp on a first trip through the Bible than some of the other biblical text. Hence, while you will find some treasures in the majors even without much background (for example, Isaiah 53, the descriptions of God in Ezekiel, etc.), some of the material will leave you scratching your head...and that's okay...for now. Remember, this is the first time you're reading through the Bible. You're looking for the big picture, the broad strokes, the context of how it all fits together. Details are important, but many of them will come later.

Whatever you do, don't be afraid of the prophets. When you're ready, jump in and start to swim. I remember being fascinated the first time I read Jeremiah. Did I understand it all? Not even close. But I was struck by the characterization of Israel, by their stiff-necked manner and unrepentant heart, and I came to a better understanding of why God was disciplining them. It wasn't for one bad choice they made. It was for bad choice after bad choice after bad choice. After my "indignant" phase with Israel, I also realized how much like them I often tend to be...and I have the benefit of the indwelling Holy Spirit, which they did not have. Let's just say, it makes you think.

14. Pay attention to the details (genealogies, etc.), but don't bog down in them now.

If you have to skim a bit on genealogies, Levitical laws, the beginning of the book of Numbers, or the end of Ezekiel, don't beat yourself up about it. Genealogies did nothing for me the first couple of times I read through the Bible, and they probably won't for you either. The funny thing is, though, the more I have come to grasp the whole of the Bible (and I still, have a long ways to go), the more the seemingly "boring" things have come into focus. Rahab, the prostitute, is in the line of Jesus—interesting. How about the prayer of Jabez squashed right there in the thick of the Chronicles? There's a worthwhile little gem.

If you happen to be a perfectionist, this may send you into a bit of a craze. After all, if you haven't really read everything, you haven't read everything. My advice: Loosen up! I know, I know, easier said than done, but just for fun give it a whirl. If you feel that guilty, next time through you can memorize the genealogies!

15. Try to ignore the chapter breaks.

The chapter and verse breaks are not inspired. And as helpful as they are in navigating the Bible, they get in the way when we read. They cause us to stop and start like a car on an urban road. Learning to ignore the chapter breaks will cause your reading to be more like an uninterrupted ride through Montana. Additionally, as you read, you'll find several places where chapter and verse breaks actually detract from meaning by grouping content away from its natural context.

16. Stay away from the footnotes.

Footnotes are well-meaning helps, but you need to stay away from them as much as possible. They are one person's view of the text you are reading. If you don't understand something, you need to go back and look at the context, not the footnotes. If you hang out in the footnotes, you'll be inadvertently buying into a theological school of thought rather than searching the Scriptures for yourself and allowing the Holy Spirit to be your teacher.

Are they helpful? Sure. Sometimes. Same thing with commentaries. They can be valuable tools after you have done the digging for yourself.

17. Read the Psalms and Proverbs concurrently with something else.

Chances are you'll love reading the Psalms and Proverbs, provided you don't try to read straight through. I highly suggest reading both of the books of poetry concurrently with something else. Sure, you can read through five or six Psalms in one sitting and learn from them how to worship. If you try to read twenty or thirty at a time, though, you'll just plain overdose. The Psalms are words that really do need to be meditated upon. Don't rush. Let them soak into your soul as you read. Pick out a favorite, memorize it, and let the Holy Spirit teach you how to worship through it.

At the same time, however, you need to realize that the Psalms total one hundred fifty. That means at a rate of one Psalm a day, it would take you nearly a half a year to get through this book. This is fine if you're also reading somewhere else at the same time, and you happen to be a plodder. Sprinters (like me) will go crazy at a Psalm a day pace. Better for us to read five to ten a day and feel great about our "chapter volume" for a bit.

The Proverbs, on the other hand, will give you good guidelines for life; short, quick little sayings that generally prove to be true if carried out. Again, they are best taken in a chapter or two a day. Otherwise, due to the brevity of the sayings, they will all simply run together in your mind. One of the bigger mistakes many people make when reading the Proverbs is believing they are actual promises of God to them. They simply are not. Yes, the Bible does contain many promises; they just are not found in the book of Proverbs. Proverbs, as said before, are life principles, which generally hold true. Important? Yes. Helpful? Absolutely. Just don't get your pants in a bunch if you think God is breaking His promises when you see a proverb not holding true. By the way, there are thirty-one chapters in the book of Proverbs. That makes it a great one-chapter-a-day read to go along with something else.

As you read, you are sure to discover some helpful techniques of your own for reading through the Bible. You will also discover areas that are particularly challenging for you. Jot these down below so that you can pass your tips on to others and remember them for yourself another time through. No sense in reinventing the wheel. Share what you have learned to spur someone else on in the faith!

Techniques that have worked for me:

1.

2.

3.

4.

5.

6.

7.

8.

9.

10.

Areas of difficulty that I have found in reading through the Bible:

1.

2.

3.

4.

5.

6.

7.

8.

9.

10.

Drawing Near

+ Read the Five-Minute Survey of the Old Testament located in the Bible Study Toolbox at the back of this book.

+ Read the Old Testament book of I Samuel (if you're familiar with stories in Genesis).

+ If you don't have any biblical or church background, read Genesis, the very first book of the Bible. By the way, don't be embarrassed if this is the category into which you fall. We all learn little by little.

+ Pick two epistles (remember, an epistle is a letter) to read this week. Remember to read an epistle in one sitting because that's how you read a letter.

+ Try reading the Minor Prophet Jonah.

+ Read to your kids from an Old Testament storybook.

+ If you don't have a children's Bible storybook in the house, buy one.

Ablaze

—3—

The Truth About Understanding

No One "Gets" Everything Right Away

ARE YOU THE KIND OF PERSON who's bothered when you don't understand something? I sure am. Drives me nuts. But I'm getting used to it. And if you want to make it through the Bible, you need to get used to it too. Don't misunderstand here. It is important to study deeply and to learn to handle accurately the Word of God as Paul tells us in his second letter to Timothy (2:15). That is imperative for disciples of Jesus Christ. One of the key principles of accurately handling the Word of God, however, has to do with keeping material in context. Context is king in matters of interpreting the Word of God. Thus, we need to READ BROAD-LY and STUDY DEEPLY because while the Bible is made up of sixty-six smaller books, it is still God's Word to man and the context of the whole helps us greatly in understanding individual parts.

So the first time you read through the Bible, don't become unduly concerned when something doesn't seem to click. Don't try to solve the timing of the rapture or become disheartened if you leave the reading of the prophets with more questions than you have answers. Realize that the more you read, the more you will "get it." The more context you have—the more Bible reading you have done, whether or not you have "gotten" it all—the easier it will be to study deeply and to put the pieces together. The converse, I believe, is also true. It is much harder to study deeply when you don't have some working knowledge of the entire corpus of Scripture. Without a strong knowledge of the context of the Bible, your vulnerability level to heresy increases dramatically. Does that really matter? Of course it does, because the most effective lies are those that are mixed thoroughly with large doses of truth.

Realize here, too, that while some would like you to believe that studying the Bible is just this side of "rocket science," it simply is not. The Bible is God's Word to man and its message is within the grasp of all. Just because some people read the Old Testament in Hebrew and can split New Testament Greek words, doesn't mean that you, by comparison, are a second class Christian. In fact, at times those who are parsing Greek verbs find they can't see the forest for the trees. In order to study the Bible, you don't need to know the meaning of exegesis or hermeneutics, eschatology or soteriology—not that they aren't fun fifty-cent words to carry around in your pocket! What you need is a heart open to God's working and the diligence to continue seeking Him.

When people think they need to understand everything right out of the box, it prevents them from ever attempting to read the Bible, or as they fail to understand what they are reading, they give up and that failure becomes an even stronger barrier to future study.

1. Understand and value the importance of context.

Context is king in reading and studying the Bible. If you get nothing else out of this book, this is the point you need to get: context is king. Without context, it is possible to make the Bible say almost anything—to preach or teach anything you choose. Everything becomes relative; everything is gray just like our world today. In truth, nothing can be understood out of context. Therefore, studying deeply without context is next to impossible unless you are relying on someone else to point you to the places in the text where similar topics come up. And that is helpful, but you will eventually want to learn how to go beyond that.

2. Agree with yourself that reading through the Bible will not be a one-time event.

Simply resolve together with God that reading through the Bible will not be a one-time "check-it-off-my-life-goal-list" kind of activity. Honestly, the minute you determine to continue reading the Word, the pressure for immediate and total understanding vanishes. Sure, if you're that "type" (and I speak as one who is), having some questions will eventually spur you on to more study, and that's great. That's what should happen. That's what needs to happen. The point here is to keep the questions from totally derailing you as you seek to gain context. You are not ignoring questions; you are taking the first step toward answering them by gaining the additional information of context and extended context.

Think for a moment of a child coming to his parent complaining that his sister hit him. The parent most certainly has questions. Where were you? What were you doing? Did she hit you for a reason? Did you do something to provoke her? Was she just being mean? Now any thinking adult realizes that before any punishment is doled out, questions need to be answered. Not only this, but questions need to be answered from a variety of sources to determine the whole story. What the parent needs is context. Little Jimmy is only going to give part of the story. Mom and Dad need the sister's story, and they need to hear from any other eyewitnesses what was going on. They need context.

The great thing about the Bible is that it always provides context. First, it provides the context of the book in which material appears, and then the context of the whole Bible. Since Scripture interprets Scripture, you'll find that difficult passages in certain areas will clear up dramatically when you read other parts of Scripture. But you have to be reading the whole Word of God to be able to use this principle effectively.

3. Get rid of the pencil.

Okay. Now I know I've offended some people. After all, telling a "pencil reader" to abandon the lead is like telling a chain smoker to go cold turkey, maybe worse. I speak here as Queen of the Pencil Readers. Understand I am not saying never read the Bible with a pencil. I do it all the time. But the first time I made it all the way through the Bible, I didn't use the pencil. If this is your first time reading through the Bible, drop the pencil with the understanding that the next time through and the time after that and the time after that you can underline all you want. By setting down the pencil, we begin to interact with the Word as a book instead of an assignment. Do you read novels with a pencil? Do you use a highlighter when you pick up a magazine? The key here is two-fold. First, we need to learn to enjoy reading the Bible, to have it be a natural "pick up." Second, we need to read the first time for the overall message to begin to see how everything holds together. The more we read, the clearer everything becomes, but if we get so bogged down in minutia the first time around, the odds that we'll make it back through a second, third, or fourth time diminish.

So, don't knock it until you try it. Drop the pencil and see if your attitude toward reading changes as mine did. No guarantees here, but give it a try.

4. Lose the overly high emotional expectations.

The earth won't move every time you read the Bible. Sometimes it will, but don't count on it every day. Some days God will seem so near that you'll hardly be able to comprehend it. Other days He'll seem distant. Just keep going. Keep putting the Word in and letting Him work on the person He wants you to become. Over time you will find God making changes in you, making you more and more like Jesus. Realize, this may be imperceptible to you at the start, but chances are that others around you will begin to notice a change and all of a sudden, you'll realize that things that used to be very important to you are not so much any more, and other things are beginning to take their places.

We get so hung up on our emotions; we want goose bumps and a certain feeling in the pit of our stomachs, but that is not what Christianity is about. It is about a confidence and hope in God; it is about a sound mind and a clean heart, not bumpy skin and warm intestines.

5. Get it in and trust God to use it.

I can't stress this one enough, particularly if you are an I-have-to-understand-everything type of person. If you are truly a child of God and seek Him through His Word, God will use that Word to affect radical change in your life. Let me say that again, God will use that Word to affect radical change in your life. This is a biggie. You obey by seeking Him, but you must realize that only He can change you, only He can give you understanding. That being the case, it is imperative that we put the Word in and allow Him to work.

6. Read broadly.

The Bible can be a tough book to grasp. Although authored by God whose message is consistent, the Bible was at the same time written through various human "authors." Thus, while the message is consistent throughout, different human authors have different styles and stress different concepts. All this to say that as you study deeply, the broad reading you do will make more sense because you are coming to understand in a more thorough way the concepts of the Bible. At the same time, the more broadly you read, the more sense you will be able to make of individual passages because you will have better understanding of the larger context.

7. Join a Bible study where you will learn to study deeply.

I can't stress this one enough. Reading through the Bible will help you to get the big picture; it will help you with context; it will help you see how things hang together. It will help you hear God, and God uses it in your lives to strengthen each of your relationships with Him. It is His Word, and His Word is truly life to us. I can't even find a way to express the importance of digesting the full counsel of God. In order to digest fully the Word of God, we need to learn how to be good students of the Word. As Paul says in 2 Timothy 2:15, we need to learn to handle accurately the Word of truth. A solid biblically based inductive study will help you in doing just this.

For some people, study is just not a good word. It is, nonetheless, vital in a growing relationship with God. A good study will help you learn to ask the right questions of the text, such as:

- Who wrote the text?
- To whom was it written?
- Why was it written?
- When was it written?
- What are the key words in the text?
- What is the theme of the book?
- What is the theme of the individual chapters?

A good study will help you learn how to do word studies to find out what nuances specific words had in their original language (Greek for the NT, Hebrew for most of the OT). No, you don't have to learn Greek and Hebrew to make use of the study tools! A good study will also help you see texts in their near and greater context and to let Scripture interpret itself. A good Bible study will not ask, "What does this mean to you?" but rather, it will help you determine what the text meant to the original hearers. Based on that determination, how it can then apply in our lives today. A Precept Ministries Bible study, for example, will teach you to ask, "Now that I've studied, how does understanding the meaning of the text apply to me?"[1] Learning to study helps to keep us from reading our own views into the text.

An excellent book on this topic is Kay Arthur's *How to Study Your Bible*.[2] It takes you step by step through the inductive study method, which will help you to learn to dig out the truths of God's Word for yourself. My favorite for in-depth Bible study is Precept Ministries International because they teach you to do just that.

8. Find a Paul.

What, you ask, is a "Paul?" A "Paul" is a mentor in the faith (someone who "disciples" to put it in biblical terms), a person who is more spiritually mature than you are, who can help you in your spiritual growth and understanding of Scripture. While we'll deal with the mentoring concept in greater depth later in this book, you need to know that a mentor can help you discern what in the Bible is most important to understand fully. Don't have a grasp on the humanity and deity of Jesus? That's a problem. Having trouble with sequencing all of the Old Testament prophecy and the eschatology of the New Testament? A good mentor will be able to help clear up some of the cloudy issues and point you in the direction of study that is going to be of most help to you in your spiritual walk.

The ultimate goal is to handle accurately the Word of truth on your own, but along the way, a mentor can be a tremendous help. A good mentor will also be helpful in calling you to task on whether or not you are applying and living out what you are reading and studying.

A good mentor will also be able to encourage you when the going gets tough. And it will get tough at times because we are in a war. Our enemy will not take our getting serious with God sitting down. I don't say this to scare you. I say this to remind you because forewarned is forearmed.

9. Learn to be an active reader.

While we're not trying to answer every question the first time through, that doesn't preclude interacting vigorously with the text and asking questions of it as you read. "Who is the writer? Why is he writing? To whom is the book addressed? Why was it written?" In order to catch what is going on, we need to train ourselves to ask questions of the text in the course of our reading to help us to see the whole picture. Just think back to the journalistic five *W*'s and the *H* to help you as you read:

+ Who is writing? To whom is it written?
+ What is he trying to say?
+ Where was he going? From where was the book written?

- Why did the author write?
- When was the book written?
- Are there any specific "How" questions that the text answers?

Eventually, you'll answer these questions on paper or in the computer as you start studying the text deeply, but for now, answer them in your head as you go along. Be a journalist; ask questions, get answers!

10. Avoid the temptation to spiritualize.

Have you ever sat in a "Bible study" (and, yes, the quotation marks are deliberate) where everyone in the group takes a turn telling what a particular passage means to them? I hope you haven't, but I'm guessing at some point you have. This is one way that we do not accurately handle the Word of truth. Yes, the Bible speaks to us today, but that speaking must come out of an understanding of what the text said to its original hearers. What it means to us must come out of what it meant. For that, sorry to be so repetitive, we need context and study.

11. Avoid the temptation to naturalize.

When we naturalize the Bible, we disallow anything that is not empirical. By empirical I mean anything that cannot be seen, measured, touched, felt, examined, or proved. According to a naturalistic view, miracles could not have happened because they do not fit the way that we know the world operates. People do not rise from the dead. Therefore, accordingly, Jesus could not have been raised from the dead; neither could He have raised others from the dead. Furthermore, we all know that those of flesh and blood cannot walk on water unless the temperature has fallen significantly below thirty-two degrees Fahrenheit. Five loaves of bread and two fish cannot feed 5,000 men, to say nothing of their dates.

Now, while many would not think of viewing the New Testament in a naturalistic way, the Old Testament is quite another story. It is not uncommon to find people who accept the miracles of Jesus, but who can't bring themselves to believe that a big fish swallowed a little man named

Jonah. Similarly, they can accept Jesus as God but can't accept that God may actually have made the earth in six days as He said.

Certainly, the Bible uses figurative language at times; the Psalms, Revelation, and the prophets are some examples. And when figurative language is used, we need to interpret the material in the manner that the author intended. However, we can't force the term "figurative" language or "allegory" on people or events that Jesus spoke of as being the real thing. If you're feeling disagreeable here, just consider what I'm saying, mark your margin and move on.

12. Avoid the temptation to dogmatize.

If you grew up in the church, you probably struggle with this problem to some degree whether or not you realize it. Dogmatizing makes the Bible agree with a view that is already held by the dogmatic person, whether or not his original view is truly scriptural. For example, you will approach the Bible differently if you believe in predestination as opposed to the free will of man. If you think you can lose your salvation, you will approach passages differently than if you believe that your salvation is eternally secure. Your church may have pet views on the rapture of the church, or baptism, or any one of a number of things. Because of the views that surround us and our own preconceived ideas, the tendency to read into the Bible what we think it says can become very great. We all have presuppositions. We need to be aware of them and keep them in check as we come to the Bible. The more we allow the Bible to speak for itself and to interpret itself, the better off we will be.

Furthermore, choosing between two opposing views or dogmas may put us on a wrong path. Some combined biblical truths (such as the sovereignty of God and the free will of man) may not make sense to us, but they do to God. By faith I accept both, let God solve the apparent dilemma, and I simply move on in my study of the Bible. We can easily get hung up on some of these "difficulties" and get sidetracked from much more important things.

We need to read the Bible the way we eat fish. When we come upon a bone, we just lift it out, lay it aside, and go on eating. When we come upon a "bone" in Scripture, we need to do the same, lay it aside and go on reading. I may find the answer further on in my study, or I may simply have to leave it with God. After all, He is omniscient, and I am not. The fact that I cannot understand some of these apparent clashes of truth helps me accept the fact that God is far greater than I am and He is worthy of my trust.

You will also find that the more you read (if you are reading with an open mind) the less you will find yourself holding onto the dogma of men. When we don't know the truth for ourselves, we often cling to the dogmas of men because we long for something that is true and stable. We'll fight for positions that we really know nothing about because we have a need for security and stability. When you get into the Word of God, though, you find the source of truth, and the dogmas of man no longer become so important. As Jesus says in the gospel of John (8:32), "And you will know the truth, and the truth will make you free."

13. Start practicing your hermeneutical leaps.

Okay, I know I said you didn't have to know what hermeneutics and exegesis are, but you do need to understand the English concepts that they stand for. Hermeneutics is just a fancy word that means the art and science of interpreting Scripture. It involves two basic steps:

+ Drawing out what the text meant to its original hearers (also called exegesis, from the Greek word meaning "to draw out").
+ Applying the text today based on what it originally meant.

Realize that while the text of Scripture can be applied in more than one way, valid application must come out of what the text meant to its original hearers in their context.

14. Apply the clear teaching and live in the light of it.

If we're honest, it is not the one percent or five percent or even ten percent of the Bible that we don't understand that poses the problem for us; it is the ninety-nine percent, ninety-five percent, or ninety percent that we do understand. Sure, we can all come up with a few perplexing scriptural references that give us fits, but how much would alternate interpretations actually affect the way we live our lives? Probably not at all.

Conversely, how differently would the visible church today look if people were into the Word of God and being transformed from the inside out into people who love the brethren, who pursue peace with all men, who let their lights shine, who walk in the light, who hold marriage in honor, who are not shackled by the love of money or by the fear of death…are you getting my point here?

How different would the church at large look if we followed Paul's instructions to Titus on how older men, older women, younger women, and younger men should live?

15. Always interpret unclear teaching in light of clear teaching, not vice versa.

I'll never forget the first time that I had to read through the book of Romans. I was in grade school and had to read the book to pass a couple of sections in my Awana Clubs' handbook. I was cruising right along until I ran into Romans 9. It was like hitting a box of bricks in the middle of a clear highway. I was lying on the red-carpeted floor of our family room, and all of a sudden, I saw what I perceived to be a different God in the pages of Scripture than the one I had been taught about my entire life. In case you've just furrowed your eyebrows with the "What's Romans 9?" look—it is a passage in which Paul refers back to Jacob and Esau, attributing to God statements such as "Jacob I loved, but Esau I hated." Was I finding a different God? No, but it was certainly a difficult passage. When I studied it in connection with the Old Testament references (as I did years later in college), it made much more sense to me. Still, it shook me for a while because instead of focusing on the clear I started looking at the unclear.

For a long time I disliked the book of Hebrews. I remember the day when our pastor announced that we would be studying the book of Hebrews on Sunday mornings and that he anticipated that the series would take about a year. It briefly ran through my mind to change churches for a year, but instead I decided to throw myself wholeheartedly into the book. By the time the year was over and I had invested quite some time in memorization, I loved Hebrews! It wasn't until very recently that I realized my former distaste probably came from a couple of sticky passages in chapters six and ten. They sounded at face value as if salvation may be lost. Again, I avoided one of my current New Testament favorites because I allowed myself to be scared off by the unclear.

16. Watch out for the trap of reading about the Bible instead of reading the Bible.

Boy, is this an easy one to fall into. I did this throughout most of college, and I still fall into this trap occasionally. Realize that reading commentaries and secondary sources provide a great deal of help in Bible study. However, the life-changing power of God comes when we directly interact with Him through His Word. Commentators, while helpful, simply are not inspired. The Bible, conversely, describes itself rightly as "God-breathed." Should you use commentaries when you are studying in-depth? Absolutely, but use them after you have done your own study, after you have wrestled with the issues in the text yourself. You will be more informed and better able to judge the value of what the commentators have to say on the passage if you have first worked through the Scriptures yourself. A couple of other points on commentaries are worth noting. First, make sure that you use more than one commentary so you can compare viewpoints. Second, take care to choose a reputable commentator, one who tells you all the alternate views of interpretation before letting you know why he has chosen his particular view. Other helps in selecting a commentary can be the advice of a pastor or teacher in your church or taking note of the company that published the book.

17. Major on the majors.

The ungodly will major on the minors. The Bible is very clear on this. Paul tells us in 2 Timothy 2:23, "But refuse foolish and ignorant speculations, knowing that they produce quarrels." The ungodly argue about genealogies and details and weird stuff. They make extra rules, make you jump through extra hoops, and generally get way off track. They make big deals out of unclear passages, building them up into major tenets of the faith while at the same time totally messing up on the major issues, specifically on the person of Jesus Christ.

18. Read history before prophecy.

If you don't understand some of the history of Israel, the prophets will be very unclear to you. So don't start in Isaiah or Jeremiah or Ezekiel or in the minor prophets. Before you read the prophets, get yourself through 1 and 2 Samuel and 1 and 2 Kings, and you'll have a much better base for "getting" the prophets. Still, they won't be crystal clear right away, so don't fret, just start to get your context.

Things You Need to Understand

Before we move on, I need to make one qualification. While you will not understand everything you read in the Bible—and that's okay for the time being—there are a few points on which you need to be absolutely clear. If you aren't, these are the ones you do need to pursue with diligence sooner than later.

1. You need to be clear on Jesus Christ.

Do you want to be sure that you have the main point of the Bible? Do you want to know that you won't be sucked in by some bizarre heresy? Then get clear on the person and work of Jesus Christ. Don't get into it with the Mormons over "baptism for the dead" or their conception of the levels of heaven. Don't fret over the 144,000 of Revelation and what the Jehovah's Witnesses believe about it. Stick to Jesus and make sure you are clear on Him. This is the point where every heretical teaching will be off. Not almost every heresy, every heresy. Sure, they'll be off in a lot of other areas, too, but this is the deal-breaker. Read the Gospels until you understand who Jesus is, the God-man, one hundred percent human, one hundred percent divine. Watch how the Old Testament points to Him. Look at the sacrificial system with a view toward the sacrifice of Jesus Christ. See how the prophets point toward Him. Build on the foundation of Jesus, get your Christology right and go from there. Start with the clear and move to the unclear. Get clear on the essentials before you start worrying about issues that people argue over.

2. You need to be clear on the gospel, the good news of Jesus Christ.

How do you get to heaven? How do you have a right relationship with God? You need to be clear on these. Most people, even those who profess to believe the Bible, think that in some fashion they have to work their way to God. This, however, is clearly not a biblical truth. The biblical truth is that Jesus did the work, not us.

The word gospel means simply "good news." Paul defines that good news in a letter to the church at Corinth. He states in 1 Corinthians 15:3–8, "For I delivered to you as of first importance what I also received, that Christ died for our sins according to the Scriptures, and that He was buried, and that He was raised on the third day according to the Scriptures, and that He appeared to Cephas [Peter], then to the twelve. After that He appeared to more than five hundred brethren at one time, most of whom remain until now, but some have fallen asleep; then He appeared to James, then to all the apostles; and last of all, as to one untimely born, He appeared to me also."

It is here in the first letter to the Corinthians that the components of the good news are very clearly spelled out for us.

+ *Christ died for our sins.* Because Jesus Christ was without sin, He could pay the penalty for our sin.
+ *He was buried.* He really died; it was not an extended fainting spell.
+ *He was raised on the third day.* When God raised Him from the dead, the power of sin and death was broken. Death cannot hold the perfect Son of God!
+ *He appeared.* People actually saw Him. It was not a mere myth or legend. Death had been defeated.

3. You need to be clear on what Christ's death means for you and me.

Okay, you may say, so He died for my sins, what practically does that mean for me? It means that we can have a right relationship with God and thereby be delivered from the power of sin and of death. It means forgiveness and peace in the here and now and life everlasting in the presence of God.

As it stands right now, if we don't have a relationship with God, we are in deep, deep trouble. We may or may not acknowledge it, but it is truth nonetheless.

The Bible says that we have sinned; we have missed the mark and have fallen short of what God requires which is absolute perfection. Specifically, it says in Romans 3:23, "For all have sinned and fall short of the glory of God." In our world, this can be a tough concept to accept since we tend to either compare ourselves to others and think we're better than they are or simply to conclude that there is no such thing as absolute truth. If truth does not exist, how then can I fall short of a standard that is not real?

The way this concept makes best sense to me is to think of a swimming race from the coast of San Diego to Hawaii. There is a definite goal: Hawaii. Now, when the gun sounds and we all jump in the water, some would make it further than others. You might make it further than me, and an Olympic distance swimmer no doubt would make it further than both of us would. But make no mistake, none of us would make it without the assistance of a boat, plane, or helicopter. The goal is not attainable, just as the perfect standard of God is not attainable by human beings, save Jesus Christ who was fully human and fully God. Some of us are better than others. Mother Teresa lived an exemplary life. Jesus, Himself, speaks highly of John the Baptist. Neither Mother Teresa nor John the Baptist, however, could match the perfection that God requires. No one comes to God except through Jesus (John 14:6).

Sorry, but before we can get to the actual good news of Jesus, the path first gets darker. That is because our sinning and falling short of God's glory comes with a consequence. The Bible calls it a wage. What we earn is death. Romans 6:23 makes this very clear when it states, "For the wages of sin is death." This is not a good place to be. It is, however, where all humanity is apart from Christ because none of us can make that swim to Hawaii without help.

Fortunately, God does not leave us here sinking, so to speak, in the middle of the Pacific Ocean of sin. Instead, He reaches out to us in our corrupted condition. Romans 5:6 says, "For while we were still helpless, at the right time Christ died for the ungodly." He brings His one-person helicopter to us in the middle of the ocean, gets into the water, and helps us safely aboard the chopper when He became man (incarnate) and died in our place.

Although Christ died for the ungodly, not all of the ungodly have accepted the gift. So, how do we practically lay hold of this cure that God has affected on our behalf?

The Bible tells us in Ephesians 2:8-9: "For by grace you have been saved through faith; and that not of yourselves, it is the gift of God; not as a result of works, so that no one may boast." The difference between intellectual assent to facts and saving faith is often illustrated by the use of a chair. You can look at a chair and believe in your mind that the chair will support your weight when you sit, but until you actually park your posterior, you have not really trusted it to sustain you.

Another illustration that works better for me comes from the team-building arena. Several years ago, my husband and I helped lead a group of high-schoolers from our church on a leadership retreat. One of the weekend activities was a team-building course where the students would learn to trust one another at a higher level. One of the activities involved putting one student on a platform with his back to his peers who were standing at ground level. The students on the ground were strategically placed and were instructed to put out their arms to make a human net to catch the student on the platform. The "lucky" one on the platform then had to fall backward off the platform into the arms of his peers who were located a distance below. Now, each of the kids knew the stunt would work; after all, if it didn't, there would be lawsuits. Still, believing in their heads that their friends would catch them and actually letting go and falling into their arms were two completely different things. The first was intellectual assent, the latter, biblical belief or trust.

Drawing Near

- Read Isaiah 1–6 and note what you learn about man and about God.

- Read Jeremiah 5–9 and note what you learn about the children of Israel. Is there anything that you as a Christian can learn from their behavior that you might be able to apply today? Did you understand everything else that was going on in this passage? If not, was the portion about obedience clear enough for you to be able to make some life application?

- Read Revelation 1–3. What do you learn about Jesus? What are some of the things that disturb Jesus about His churches? Are there sound applications you can make from these chapters even without knowing for sure what some of the details refer to? Why or why not?

- Read the book of Daniel. While much of the prophetic sections may not be immediately clear, what clear lessons can you learn from this book about God and the lives of those who follow Him fully?

- Read through one of the Gospels without a pencil (Matthew, Mark, Luke, or John) and just let yourself be with Jesus.

- Read an epistle with the five *W*'s and *H* in mind and as you're reading, keep asking, "What is the take away? How can I apply this to my life today?"

- If you're still in a twit about the "drop the pencil" comment (yes, I know some of you are), go out and buy yourself a nice notebook, then label it "My Question Journal for Later Study." You can record all the major burning questions that you just have to have answered. As you continue reading through the Bible, you'll be able to come back and glance at the journal to see just how many of the questions have been answered through your reading of other parts of Scripture.

—4—

The Truth About Time

Perfect Time Does Not Exist

IS SOLITUDE WITH GOD IMPORTANT? Absolutely. Whatever you do, don't read here that time alone with God is not important; it is essential. Followers of Christ know this. We know that we need time to commune with our God. Look at the life of Jesus. He was God incarnate, and yet He spent much of His time in solitude communing with His heavenly Father. We don't always do it, but we know that we need to. The problem is that in the evangelical community, at least, we have this term called "quiet time" that we associate with about a fifteen-minute time slot, a devotional (or if we're doing really well an actual Bible), and the absence of other people. In the Old Testament, which was given for our instruction and example, according to the apostle Paul, we see that the people were instructed to meditate continuously on the Law, the Word of God they had at the time. God instructs Joshua (1:8) saying, "This book of the law shall not depart from your mouth, but you shall meditate on it day and night, so that you may be careful to do according to all that is written in it; for then you will make your way prosperous, and then you will have success." The Hebrew word translated "meditate," means literally, "to mutter." We can't mutter out of our mouths words that are not in our heads and hearts.

As I grow in Christ, God draws me into more and more solitude and on a more regular basis very early in the morning. However, as I began seriously reading the Word earlier in life, it was a very different affair. Back in the day, when my body could still bounce back, my solitude happened almost exclusively at night anywhere from 10 p.m. to 12 midnight (and later). That doesn't work for my old body anymore, but it once did. God has worked with me in different ways at different times.

Thinking that we have to have the perfect time to spend with God presents a real challenge, especially for Westerners who have become accustomed to filling every moment of every day. If we believe that we have to have perfect "quality" time, many people simply will never make the effort to read God's Word. The laundry is never done, the floor is never clean enough, the room is never quiet enough to rest and read. We have guilt if we read in less than perfect conditions. Sure, we can deny it, but other things call our names, other things that are important. Hey, if I had a housekeeper (or was a better one myself), this book would have been finished two years ago.

I'd like to suggest a new paradigm here: "I will give God not only 'quality' time, but 'quantity' time." We use this term when we talk about our kids, so why not God as well? If our kids deserve quantity, how about God? And as His children, how much better off are we if we spend not only quality, but also quantity time with Him?

1. Realize that time spent is a priority issue.

We all have twenty-four hours in a day with the exception of a couple of people in the Old Testament whose days were extended. Thus, to say that you simply do not have time to read through the Bible when others can find the time comes down to a matter of priority. Sure, some have fewer responsibilities than others, but we all have the choice of our priorities. Let me illustrate…

Let's say I offered you $1,000 cash if you would read just ten pages of your Bible today. Do you suppose that you could find the time? If I showed up on your doorstep every afternoon at 1:00 p.m. with $1,000 cash for having read just ten pages of your Bible that day, how many days a week do you surmise that you would miss? Now if, perchance, you made it in the technology sector and got out in time and $1,000 doesn't make the illustration work for you, substitute your own number that would. Yes, the illustration is extreme. I trust that you do, however, see the point. We can make the time for anything for which we want to make the time. To say that you "just don't have the time" to read your Bible means that you are too busy. Plain and simple. Remember, I said up front that this book was not going to be about political correctness. You choose how you spend your time. Do it wisely.

2. Read in front of your children.

For a big part of the population, caring for children (especially small children) is an easy excuse for not reading the Bible. Little ones seem to be omnipresent. Toddlers are everywhere all of the time. It doesn't matter how early I get up in the morning because my children will wake up ten minutes later. Some of you understand this totally. Those who have never lived with children may not. And those whose children are grown and gone have often experienced some repression in this area, having forgotten how grueling the preschool years can be!

Truth be told, I'm probably a contemplative at heart—put me in a quiet room with my Bible and God, and I'm set. But I have children, very talkative ones—and dogs, a very old but "barky" Dalmatian and a couple of Great Dane puppies—and a husband. So much for the contemplative lifestyle.

Here's the point: some of us have circumstances in life that make it easier for us to pursue actual "quiet" with God. Others have circumstances that could prevent us from having a quiet time. I prefer to read in dead quiet, but because of my season of life, I've had to learn to read with PBS in the background, with boys running through the house yelling, and with a dog announcing every car coming down our street. Yes, I do read in the quiet sometimes. I need to. In fact, recently, God has been waking me earlier and earlier and making this a new habit. But if I'm looking for real quantity, I have to bloom where I'm planted, so to speak, and in the presence of those who are planted around me.

A funny thing happened to me as I started reading the Bible in front of my kids. Something I never would have expected. They wanted to join in with me. A few years ago, I read through the Bible on my laptop computer. As I read, I marked key words and phrases with different colors and symbols. My then nine year old thought this was just cool beyond belief. Who would have known? Of course, whatever the older one does, the younger one has to do too (her nickname around these parts is "Me Too!"). So as I'd point to the words on the screen that needed to be marked, she'd click the mouse and giggle. Don't think I'm going to try to tell you that I read with the same comprehension when I'm being "helped." I don't, but I do gain more than if I hadn't read at all. The bigger benefit here, though, is letting my kids see how important the Bible is to me and giving them the opportunity to experience "fun" in Bible study. Sure pointing and clicking was mainly at familiar words, but they began associating the Bible with something enjoyable. My son even picked out "joy" as a key word in Philippians. Who'd have thought? As I read, I'm able to explain some of what I am reading to them, not out of a devotional or a storybook, but directly out of God's Word, which is where I want them to be able to go on their own someday soon.

Of course, I did run into a little trouble the other day when my daughter wanted me to read her the VeggieTales story of "Lyle the Kindly Viking" out of my Bible...but I digress.

3. Read to your children.
Read to them from your Bible, simplifying the tough words. Read to them from children's Bibles; get them Bible videos on DVD...whatever it takes. Make it a family affair. When they understand how important the Bible is, they'll probably be more understanding when you want to take

some time to read the Bible for yourself. No promises, but give it a try! And always remember your responsibility to teach what you are learning to your children. In fact, if you can't justify the time you personally spend reading the Bible, you can justify it for them. This year, the kids and I are going to read through *The Message* together. Yes, I'm going to skip the long genealogies, and I'll summarize Leviticus in a sentence or two, and we'll leave Song of Solomon for another day. Still, they'll have the chance to hear the guts, the thru storyline, of the whole Word for themselves.

4. Don't be afraid to read in front of others.

Now when I say read in front of others, I don't mean sit on the corner of your street like the Pharisees of old and make a big deal of being "religious" and reading your Bible. But if you have time to read and you happen to be around other people, don't feel stupid about reading your Bible. Now you may protest, "I would never feel embarrassed about reading my Bible." Maybe you're a bigger person than I am, but I have to tell you that when I have my Bible out in public sometimes I do feel a little self-conscious. I'm not entirely sure why. Sometimes, I think I'm afraid people will perceive that I think I'm better than they are. Other times, I'm afraid someone will actually ask me about my faith. Sometimes, I fear that I'll just look weird. You'll probably have some of those thoughts, too, when you first grab your Bible and read when you're waiting to pick up the kids at school or sitting in the doctor's office or whatever. My advice: If you'll be "reading out" a great deal, invest in a discreet, cool, smaller Bible that is easy to carry yet has a very readable type. Soon, you'll pick it up as quickly as you pick up your cell phone, keys, or purse...hey, if your purse is big enough, it may fit right in. My husband and dad now have the Bible on their PDAs. I'm not quite into the new millennium yet, but they sure love it, and it might work for you too!

What if reading in public leads to conversations? This could happen. But guess what! You don't have to have all the answers. Unfortunately, many people never share the faith they have because they are afraid that they will not be able to answer all of the questions that a potential skeptic could ask them. Realize, though, that a skeptic can always ask more questions than a wise person can answer. That, however, does not make the arguments of the skeptic valid. If you are a Christian and someone asks you a question about the Bible, the key issue to talk about is the person and work of Jesus Christ. This is the point of the Bible. You don't have to have the answers for the creation/evolution debate or the dating of the age of the earth, the current existence of Noah's ark, the veracity of the story of Jonah, or the like. You need to be clear that God made man, loves man, and sent Jesus, who was fully God and fully man to die on the cross in our place so that we could be forgiven of our sins and be reconciled to a holy God who could not accept us in our sinful state. The other things are important, but you don't have to have all the answers. You answer for the faith that is in you...and that answer has to do with Jesus and what He has done in your life.

5. There are times when you need QUIET.

As I write this manuscript, it is now summer vacation at my house. We have no morning obligations, and I've tried a new plan for quiet. I make sure that I am the first one awake in the house to allow myself some quiet reading time. Then, as soon as the first child wakes up, I let that child know that the house is going to be quiet for a certain amount of time, generally ranging from a half an hour to an hour, depending on how much I've already been able to read. It has worked pretty well, and I hope it is teaching my kids to learn silence—something that is in rapid decline in our culture. They are allowed to play quietly, read, go back to sleep, whatever they want as long as they are quiet and allow Mom to have her time with God. If you live alone, you will have a much easier time achieving quiet, but even if you don't, you can encourage those you live with to practice the discipline of silence for at least a short time every day. I'm still working on this one, but I'm confident it can be done!

6. Opt for quantity of time.

It is as though we feel we will dishonor God if we don't have the perfect conditions for reading His Word. We're looking here at the old quality time versus quantity time issue. Let's think about a human illustration here for a minute. Generally speaking, is a small child better off with ten minutes of quality time with a parent once a day, or by being in the presence of the parent all day through the ups and downs of life? Please don't misunderstand; I am not saying that you do not need solitude with God. If Jesus needed it, then you and I surely do. Still, we often think that the only time we can read the Bible is when we are alone with God. This is just not the case, so we need to think differently!

Think what would happen if you only talked to your spouse or your children or your best friend under perfect conditions. What would happen? Maybe I'm wrong, but I'm thinking the relationship wouldn't end up being that great. So, absolutely find time alone with God but also bring your Bible with you to the doctor's office, to lunch, to the beach. And no, it is not a sin to read in the bathroom.

Put the Word of God into your heart and mind whenever and wherever you can. Don't forego quality time alone with Him, but give Him quantity of time too. He deserves it. You will be shocked at the difference this can make in your life.

7. List your encumbrances.

In Hebrews 12:1–2, the author tells us, "Therefore, since we have so great a cloud of witnesses surrounding us, let us also lay aside every encumbrance and the sin which so easily entangles us, and let us run with endurance the race that is set before us, fixing our eyes on Jesus, the author and perfecter of faith, who for the joy set before Him endured the cross, despising the shame, and has sat down at the right hand of the throne of God."

I recently taught through the book of Hebrews and while I was doing that, God got very serious with me about the encumbrances in my life. Unlike sin, which really is a matter of black and white, encumbrances can be very difficult to identify because they are not necessarily in themselves wrong or bad. Sometimes encumbrances are actually good things that nonetheless keep us from pursuing the best.

Here are some of the things over which I was convicted:

Too much stuff – If you're not what author Sandra Felton, author of *The Messies Manual*, would term a "messie," chances are you won't connect with this, but that's okay, bear with me.[3] My house was simply loaded with too much stuff. Sentimental stuff, stuff of memories, but stuff nonetheless. The stuff took too much time to deal with, too much energy. It was always a problem lurking in the back of my mind and finally I realized that the stuff was not just a physical issue, but that it had taken on definite spiritual dimensions. It was an encumbrance I needed to throw off if I was going to run light for God.

Exhaustion entertainment – Honestly, there are times at the end of the day where I'm too tired to read deeply, to study, or to write. I feel the need to be awake and to be alone, but I am so wiped that I can't do anything productive with the time. So I channel surf, stay up later than I should, and wake up even more tired the following morning, perpetuating the cycle.

8. Lay aside the encumbrances.

Sometimes, we have to lay old things down to pick up newer and better things. Think with me for a moment of a person weighed down with bags full of garbage. They're wrapped on all his fingers, balanced on his shoulders, and draped over his forearms. The man with his garbage suddenly discovers a beautiful treasure chest, spilling over with precious jewels. The man cannot carry the garbage and the treasures, so he must choose to lay down the garbage if he wants to pick up the treasure. We do this all the time. We are so busy with all of our commitments and our stuff, but if we are to have the treasure, we must set the baggage (garbage) aside. We can't do everything, but so often we make the wrong choices. We don't have time for the Word, but we do have time for the newspaper. We can't participate in a Bible study, but we're taking a class at the local college. Or, and I love this one, "I'd love to join that Bible study, but Monday night is my standing hair appointment," or "Jimmy's soccer game," or "my favorite television show," or you fill in the blank.

9. Redeem the time.

In other words, buy back time that is currently being misused or wasted. Always have your reading Bible handy. Always! You never know when you might have a couple of minutes to read. Sure, it will be a little tough making this into a habit, but women carry purses everywhere, right? And men almost always have pockets big enough to carry a small Bible. You'll get used to it. It's helpful, I think, to have a Bible with a zipper cover so you can throw a pencil inside and always be ready to mark off your table of contents. For years, I carried my leather-bound Bible with a pencil stuck in the page where I was reading. Convenient, yes, but not so great on the binding.

10. Get a portable Bible.

Before you pick up that tattered old King James Version and jump in, it's important to remember that you will be spending at least sixty hours with this book on the first pass, so it's important to find not only the right translation but also the right style of Bible for your needs.

Bible Style. Bible style? In other words, you need to decide if you are best suited to a small Bible that you can carry around with you everywhere, to a hard back that can take the abuse of, say, small children, or something else. The traditional leather Bible certainly will set you back a couple of dollars, but it will also stand up to a bunch more abuse than a paperback.

Translation. The key here is to find a translation based on the original languages. Although odds are you have a King James Version of the Bible sitting around your house somewhere (and you may be tempted to be frugal and read it), that is one version you'll want to avoid your first time through the Bible simply because the reading will be almost as difficult as Shakespeare. It was translated for people of another era, and it is just plain tough. The *New King James*, however, is excellent, and compares favorably to my personal favorite, the *New American Standard Bible*. The *New American Standard Bible* is very true to the original languages and is, in my opinion, unparalleled as a study Bible. However, it can be a little more difficult to read. New on the scene in the word for word translations is the *English Standard Version*. It's garnering good press and is the version that I'm currently reading through. For a first time read through the Bible, though, I would recommend either the *New Living Translation* or the *God's Word Translation*, both of which are extremely reader-friendly.

There are many good translations out there, and throughout your lifetime, you'll make it through several of them. Really, you will. As you read, you'll find that you like some better than others, and you may find that you like certain translations for studying and others for your more casual reading. That's normal. I love the *New Living Translation* and the *God's Word Translation* for the Old Testament particularly because they make the prophets more understandable. However, when it comes to the New Testament, I actually find more "modern" translations a little tougher to read because I am so familiar with the *New American Standard Bible* and *New International Version* renderings of the text. The *New Living Translation*, for instance, has a little different cadence to it, which simply slows me down. Read different versions each time through, and you'll find on your own which works best for you.

Print size. Finally, you'll want to make sure that the size of the print is comfortable for you to read. While you may prefer to carry a smaller Bible, this may not be practical if the type size causes eyestrain. If you need larger type, consider purchasing a larger Bible with big type to leave at home for your reading and carry a smaller one with you when you will only be looking at limited references.

11. Try the Bible on CD or MP3 and don't rule out multi-tasking.

I have yet to do this, as I love the written word, but my husband is a Bible-on-iPod-guy. As a person with diabetes, he has to exercise everyday, like it or not. So he's started listening to the New Testament as he works out, redeeming the time. I'm thinking that this audio deal would probably work in the car, or maybe while I'm cleaning house. Sure, the quality of input may vary, but at least we are picking up something. We will never get the whole deal at once. It is always going to be as Isaiah 28:10 says, "…precept upon precept…line upon line…here a little, and there a little…" (KJV).

12. Memorize.

Okay, I know, memorizing isn't exactly going to help you get through the Bible faster, but it is a definite way to start taking the Word with you wherever you go. The more you memorize and meditate on the Word, the more God will use it to transform you, and the greater your desire for that Word that He has given you will be. Start with relevant verses, and don't rule out memorizing a chapter or even a book of the Bible. You'll be amazed at what you see when you dig that far and meditate that deeply on God's Word.

I know, I know, you've never been able to memorize, you're too old, or whatever. I'm not buying that excuse. Anyway, consider this one! I personally know people who have memorized entire books of the Bible. So it can be done.

13. Photocopy.

Sure, hauling an average-sized Bible around is not always the most convenient thing to do, but who can't fold up a few pieces of paper and throw them in a purse or back pocket? Seriously, run over to your local office supply store and copy the book of Romans. It will probably cost you all of fifty cents and you can have your text with you literally anywhere. Or get the Bible on CD or find it on a website and print off the books you are reading.

14. Change your default position.

Your computer defaults to certain settings, and if you're honest, you'll admit that you do too! I certainly do!

You need to identify your defaults (or should I say "encumbrances") and then start to substitute the Bible for your current default positions. For example:

◆ ***Substitute your Bible for other reading material.*** I love to read *Sports Illustrated*. Yes, I'm aware that it's not a typical "chick" magazine, but I love it. Used to come on Thursdays, now it comes on Wednesdays. I only care about the real sports (Cubs baseball, Bulls basketball, and Bears football), but the writing in SI is so sublime that if I'm not careful, I'll find myself twelve pages into a sixteen-page article on synchronized swimming before I even know what's happened. Anything wrong with that? Not really. Could I do better? Of course. Everyone knows that synchronized swimming isn't even a sport! Now, now, everyone's entitled to his or her opinions on these things. Right?

You see while there's nothing wrong with reading *Sports Illustrated*, I need to take care that it doesn't become my "default" read. We all know what a default position is: it's what happens when nothing intentional is happening. For instance, let's say I happen to find myself at home alone at lunchtime (a rarity, I might add). Default for me is to make a salad, pour a diet pop, find something chocolate, sit in the "big chair" and read. If the SI is around and I am not being intentional about my choices, I will pick it up. If it's a Wednesday or Thursday, there's usually still something of real interest to me in the magazine. By the following Tuesday, however, I'm reading about motor sports or figure skating or some other non-sport, just because it's there.

There are times, though, when I'm in the zone, and weeks of magazines will go unread because I've effectively changed my default position.

+ *Substitute your Bible for television.* Okay, this one may hurt a little. Do you have a show that you just have to watch? Do you have two or maybe three? I mean, you'd just die if you missed it? If you're not this shallow, then skip to the next section. For the rest of us who are honest, there is hope. Breaking the television habit can be one of the most revolutionary changes you can make in your walk with Christ...but if you're addicted, realize this is a fight you won't win on your own; you will only do it through His power. We've all heard it said that everyone has the same twenty-four hours in a day, but if you're a television addict, realize that you may be pressed for time because you are actually functioning on an adjusted twenty-hour day or worse.

Don't get me wrong here. I'm not trying to say that television is the evil empire and that we should all go back to the non-picture box days. I like a good drama or football game as much as the next person...maybe more.

Still, I've seen in my own life the correlation between my reading habits and television watching. Very simple, actually. More reading, less television...more relaxation and peace of mind. More television, less reading...more stress from not getting things done, more chaos, more guilt. One of the great lies of television is that of detachment and relaxation.

Let's face it, when you sit down to watch a drama, for example, you can temporarily disengage from your present reality, bringing short-lived relaxation. Sometimes, though, it actually keys you up more if you are drawn into the conflict of the story because all good stories have conflict! Have you ever noticed that it is exponentially more difficult to turn a television off than to turn it on? I often find that when I sit down to watch one sixty-minute show I'm often dropping a good two to two and a half hours before I even realize the time is gone.

So, how to solve this problem? The obvious solution is to turn the box off. I know, easier said than done. My less-than-spiritual suggestion is to break the habit during reruns. Again, this may not qualify for the spiritual suggestion of the year award, but if you're truly addicted, the time when it is easiest to tune out is during reruns. As you tune out the shows you have already seen, you begin to build a habit of not watching that will be easier to maintain as the regular season rolls around. Will this make it easy? No. But it will work. Pray for the endurance and power to break the habit and then schedule other appointments during those times. Go out for coffee with a friend, schedule a racquetball court or go shopping. You may be able to pick up your Bible during that time, but chances are, you're better off to schedule something out of the house as you begin changing the behavior.

+ ***Substitute your Bible for video games.*** If you have just rolled your eyes because you cannot figure out at all why someone would ever play a video game, please proceed to the next section. If you're like me, read on. One word: Tetris. Two more words, Space Invaders. Here's another: Pikmin. Laugh if you will, but if you're going to save the world with Space Invaders, you'd better clear forty-two minutes to an hour if you are as good as me! Of course, unless you really watch the clock, the time will just vaporize and you won't even realize how long you've been sitting there. If you're a Windows user, chances are you're also at least slightly addicted to Free Cell. Anything wrong with it? No. But it can swallow time if you're not mindful.

+ ***Substitute your Bible for the Internet.*** My on-line service tells me exactly how many minutes I have spent on-line when I sign off. More often than not, I'm appalled. What seems like ten minutes is often closer to an hour. Sure, it's flashy and fun, but the Internet drains time (and often morals) with the best of them.

15. Places you can take your Bible, but probably don't.
1. The bathroom
2. The tub
3. The doctor's office or anywhere else you might have to wait
4. A restaurant or cafeteria
5. The beach
6. On vacation
7. Poolside

And yours. . .

8.

9.

10.

11.

12.

13.

14.

15.

16. If God wakes you up, get up; if God keeps you up, listen to Him, not Oprah.

I find that when I sense a loss of intimacy and quiet with God, when my soul is craving quiet and my life is loud, God has an uncanny knack of waking me a little before five in the morning. When this happens, my natural tendency is to turn over and go back to sleep because I know my charges are being re-energized. But I find that is always the wrong choice. If God wakes you up, get up and meet with Him. Similarly, when the house quiets at night and you find yourself overly awake, I promise you'll find more wisdom in the Word of God than you ever will on the late news, infomercials, or even Oprah rebroadcasts!

17. Go on a personal retreat.

Several years ago, on a retreat for adult leaders of our church's high school ministry, our youth pastor had an interesting afternoon planned for all of his volunteer staff. He sent us out for two hours. Each person took only himself and his Bible and spent the next two hours alone with God out in the field, in the woods, or wherever, just so long as they had solitude. Leaving the meeting area, the faces told the story of many individuals. "Two hours? What on earth am I going to do for two hours alone with just my Bible?" At the end of the weekend, however, person after person shared how those same two hours were unexpectedly, by far, the highlight of the weekend. Now I know what you're thinking; this must not have been a very fun group. Quite the contrary. We had all worked together for years and had great fun playing together on these leadership retreats, and yet when it came down to it, the two hours of solitude allowed God to break into lives in very significant ways.

Taking solitude a step further, you may wish to go away to a retreat center or a local house of prayer for an overnight or a weekend. In the Chicago-area where I live, there is a small house of prayer run by a group of Catholic Sisters and located in one of the southwestern suburbs. I've never experienced quiet on the scale that I do there. The accommodations are very homey. Each of the six rooms has a single bed, a reading chair and lamp, a small desk, and a sink. The six rooms share two full and immaculately clean bathrooms. For meals, you can choose to bring food back to your room or share meals with the sisters. It is simply a wonderful place to be alone with God. The Sisters welcome Catholics and Protestants alike, and focus on what we have in common which is so much greater than the areas in which we differ.

18. Learn QUIET.

You may just have the problem of avoiding quiet. Think about how our society works today. We avoid quiet at all costs. We have televisions not only in the living room or the family room but often in bedrooms too. We have radios and CD players in our houses and our cars. We even carry them on our bodies. Background music is everywhere. Where do you think the term "elevator" music came from? Why on earth do we need music for a trip in an elevator?

Think about your own habits, what is the first thing you do when encountered with quiet? Do you reach for the remote, for the phone, for the radio? Most of us do. It's the culture in which we have been raised, and it flies in the face of learning solitude.

19. Learn to block noise.

You can learn to block noise. It is not easy, but it can be done. Right now, I'm writing with the *Wild Thornberrys* in the background. Sorry, if that's not good enough for you, but that's my life! When I was in high school, my now husband, who was my boyfriend at the time, was a sound engineer for a Christian rock band. I spent the better part of one summer sitting in a sound studio with rock and roll blaring...and I mean blaring... reading *Gone with the Wind*. Sure, it was a little tough at first, but I learned to focus on the text and ignore the background sound, loud as it was.

My son, however, cannot do his math homework with his sister so much as whispering in the background. Somehow, I think it's just a hang-up with not wanting to do the homework. Just a guess.

20. Ice cream and the Chicago Cubs.

I am a die-hard Cubs fan. (If you don't live in Chicago, you can't fully understand.) Anyway, a treat in our house during the middle of the summer is to stay up late when the Cubbies are playing on the west coast and eat ice cream while we ignore bedtimes and watch baseball. My four-year-old daughter was turning into a huge baseball fan over the summer. She absolutely loved the Cubs...I thought. But as we made our way into autumn and the Cubs were no longer playing, I came to realize that it was not so much my beloved Cubbies, but her beloved ice cream. We had a Pavlovian response going on. Ice Cream...Baseball...Ice Cream... Baseball. Stick with me here.

If you really hate to read, why not set up a Pavlovian response. Make your reading time a real treat. Sit in your favorite chair with your favorite treat if that's what it takes to get yourself going. Who's to say you can't set up a system of Bible...Ice cream...Bible...Ice cream. Associate your reading with something enjoyable if reading itself is not enjoyable to you. Shallow? Probably, but it could just work! Hey, it wouldn't surprise me that my daughter may just be the first female shortstop in the major leagues due to the ice-cream connection!

Drawing Near

+ Make a point to read your Bible in a public place sometime this week.

+ Sometime this week, read during a time of noise or commotion.

+ Make a positive connection (i.e. coffee, ice cream, comfy chair, etc.) and read one of the Gospels that you haven't read recently (Matthew, Mark, Luke, or John).

+ Make a substitution for a television show, magazine, newspaper, or novel and read a book of the Bible that you can finish in one sitting.

+ Pray and ask God to reveal your encumbrances. As He does, make a list and start dealing with them one at a time.

+ Select a verse or passage to memorize. Copy it by hand or photocopy it and keep it with you at all times during the week.

+ Make a point to carry your Bible with you all week.

— 5 —

The Truth About Schedules

It's About a Relationship, Not a Syllabus

THERE IS, IN MY ESTIMATION, nothing much more depressing than having a perfect schedule and falling behind. I don't know about you, but I'm great at making complex and meticulous lists and terrible about keeping them. The planning is fun, but the doing is a drag, which probably accounts for the reason I can't follow other people's Bible reading schedules. Not only do you have to "do it," you don't even have the fun of planning it! Miss a day, and you're forever trying to catch up. The reading piles up like unattended laundry in a house full of dirty young boys. Maybe you are a schedule-keeper. Maybe you can read exactly what you're told to read every day for 365 days. I'm guessing you're not, however, since you're reading this book! If you are a schedule keeper, though, there are plenty of good ones out there to follow. You're now dismissed. Find a schedule and enjoy a Book much more edifying than this one!

For those of you who are left, I have some great news! You don't need a schedule to read through the Bible! In their defense, schedules do help some people. People like me, however, they simply frustrate.

The lie of the syllabus sets up so many well-intentioned people for failure and guilt, and moves the reading of God's Word rapidly into the academic realm instead of the relationship realm. Instead of thinking, "I have to read X number of chapters a day," try thinking, "I have the privilege of spending one-on-one time with the God of the universe every day." Here are a few other suggestions to help you break out of syllabus-based thoughts and actions.

1. Remember that it's a relationship.

We've talked about this a little already, but the importance bears repeating. How do your relationships hold up when you ignore them? Sure, there are some relationships that you can put on hold occasionally that don't suffer, but just think what life would be like if you went through the day ignoring, for example, your spouse, your son, or your daughter. Even the dog gets bent out of shape if she doesn't get her fair share of time. Why do we think that we can maintain a right relationship with our God if we do not invest time with Him? In fact, a relationship with God should be the primary relationship of our lives. It's the one that provides the glue for all other relationships. I have the power to love my husband and children in a much greater fashion when God is my first love. Second place to God is much higher than first place without Him.

2. Don't let yourself get too academic.

As I mentioned, one of the main reasons I dislike Bible reading schedules is that they move the reading into the academic realm. Now, you need to understand here that I love the academic realm. I am a student at heart, always have been. We encounter problems, though, when we get so academic with the Bible that we divorce it from application. Knowledge and study without prayer and application puffs up. So study and learn but never without praying and applying what you learn to your life, or you run the risk of becoming puffed up with dead doctrine.

3. Make "appointments" with God and accept if He takes the initiative.

There are times in my life when pursuing time with God becomes incredibly difficult. When we are too busy, we need to make "appointments" with God. Just as you would set a time on the calendar for a dear friend, mark out a time when you can meet with God uninterrupted. Put it on the calendar and don't schedule over it. At times of crisis, when you feel your soul starving for God, be aware when He takes the initiative. I've had times of intense busyness when I've been crying out to God for time to meet with Him. Times when I've felt the intense need to sit quietly in His presence but have had screaming toddlers and other responsibilities from which I simply could not divest myself. I've found that at times like these when I've been crying out to God for time to spend with Him that I have then been awakened in the middle of the night or very early in the morning—I mean really awake (which I never am naturally—at least not in the past twelve years!). The first time this happened, I went for about three nights running, waking up and just being annoyed before I finally suspected that God was answering my prayer for time alone with Him. Although I had been thinking more along the lines of my husband taking the kids out for the day, God, apparently, had another way of providing the quiet time that I needed. I just didn't quite "get it" at first.

4. Even better, make general habits.

Before I say anything else, I need to say this: I need work here. I usually do read every day, but the time when I read over the years has varied like the snowflakes. I tell myself that this is because of my stage in life and that it will get better when my kids get older, and honestly, I think it will. God has been working lately in this area. The fact that my time of day varies sets me up for potential problems, the biggest of which is that God can simply be pushed out by fatigue if I haven't read my Bible before the end of the day. Being a night owl, I often do read late when the house quiets down, but sometimes I have simply had it all sucked out of me by then.

A good friend and mentor of mine who has a set "time of day" explains that she would no sooner leave the house in the morning without having spent time with God, than she would leave the house without taking a shower, brushing her teeth, or combing her hair. That is the direction I have sensed God moving me—toward more of an early-to-bed, early-to-rise mentality.

Maybe this concept will connect with you, especially if you're the "I-can't-leave-the-house-without-my-makeup" type. Personally, if I'm clean and I have a baseball cap, I'll go just about anywhere if push comes to shove, which obviously demonstrates my issues with routine, but God is still working on me in having a set appointment with Him.

5. Set a final goal and give yourself a reward.

Rewards. Does this sound really unspiritual to you? Probably so. Let's face it, sometimes a little incentive can make you move. Rewards work for kids, right? Why? Because rewards are fun! They give you the incentive to put things in gear. Several years ago after my second baby, I had held on to several extra pounds, and I was not alone. Three of my friends were also struggling to lose post-baby weight. Instead of suffering alone, we set up a little accountability group and contest. First one to take off ten pounds would win a pot of about fifty dollars. Now it wasn't that much money, but just the game of it, the potential reward, kept a bunch of chocolate out of my mouth. It kept me drinking my water and exercising four days a week.

Now, I'm encouraging rewards simply because they work. Did you realize, though, that the concept is entirely biblical? Not that we work to get to heaven or that God gives us every temporal desire. You'll quickly find out that isn't the biblical way. But throughout both the Old and New Testaments, we find God talking about rewards. As early as Genesis 15:1, we see God telling Abram, "Do not be afraid, I am a shield to you, your very great reward" (NIV). Later, in one of the most famous of biblical chapters, the so-called faith chapter in Hebrews, we read that the one who comes to God must believe "that He is and that He is a rewarder of those who seek Him." We see, too, in Hebrews 11:6 that Moses followed God and gave up the passing pleasures of Egypt because he was looking to the reward. God is a rewarder. You'll see this when you read.

So set a reward for finishing, and make it worth attaining. How about a leisurely weekend away or maybe a shopping excursion for something special. Be sure to make the treat something that you want, and don't let yourself have it until you do the job.

6. Set checkpoints with mini rewards.

The only thing that works better than big rewards are little rewards along the way!

So why not give yourself some little treats when you make progress in your Bible reading? It doesn't need to be anything big...just enough to keep you going. Maybe you'll treat yourself to dinner out with a friend, or maybe you'll treat yourself to a new blouse or an espresso. Who knows, maybe it will even be that great Greek-based, hard-back commentary on Hebrews at your local seminary bookstore that you couldn't break down and spend the $39.95 on before! Okay, or maybe not...whatever works for you. Just make it fun! Now, will you have to treat yourself for the rest of your life to keep you reading the Bible? Hopefully not. This is just one of those ways to train yourself and make it fun to get into the habit of the Bible.

Make sure that you have treats set up for finishing Leviticus, Numbers, each one of the big prophets (Isaiah, Jeremiah, Ezekiel), Acts, and Revelation.

7. Don't set a chapter per day quota.

Whatever you do, don't set a chapter per day quota. Okay, I know that most of you will pull out a calculator to do the math, so let me save you the time. To make it through the Bible in a year, you'll need to average about three chapters a day. However, please, please, please don't read three chapters a day, or you'll miss the flow and risk turning a beautiful relationship into an assignment. Read logical portions. Stop at the end of an epistle, read through the conclusion of a story, don't just stop because you've "done your time." I think back to when my son was in the second grade. Each day, he had to read for thirty minutes. At the outset, it didn't matter if he was mid-sentence when the timer went off, HE WAS FINISHED. Reading was a chore, and all he wanted was to be done!

One day, however, he asked if he could read a joke book for his reading time. I told him that he could read the back of a ketchup bottle if he wanted to, he just had to read! This revolutionized his reading time. Since then, he has learned to enjoy reading (well, some of the time).

8. Read in "chunks."

Slow and steady may win the race, but reading a couple of minutes a day is not how we read most books. So why should we read the Bible any differently? One of the best ways to "connect" with what you are reading is to set aside a couple of hours and just go at it. Think about how hard it is to get into a novel when you only let yourself read one page. Same thing with the Bible. So much of it is narrative, and it just doesn't lend itself to ten-minute reads. You'll be amazed at what God will do if you just set aside two hours of time to spend alone with Him and His Word.

This is an especially good idea if you're just starting out with a serious reading program. Take the time to immerse yourself in the Word and to rid yourself of the fear that you can't do it. When you get right down to it, isn't that half the problem, the fear that you'll start and fail?

Here are some typical books I like to read when I'm "chunk" reading:

+ Historical books: Genesis; Joshua and Judges; 1 and 2 Samuel; 1 and 2 Kings; Ezra and Nehemiah.
+ Prophetic books: Daniel and Revelation
+ Any of the Gospels
+ The book of Acts

Reading in chunks also helps us to stop looking at the clock. What is it about clocks that is so fascinating anyway?

9. Read in logical progressions.

As you read, you will tend to find that certain books lead to other books. When you find certain books linking to others, follow the chain. You may not be able to figure these out the first time you read through, but the more you read, the more you will discover strands of thought that will lead you from one book to another. The first time I read through the Bible, for instance, I started in 1 Samuel, this led to 2 Samuel and then to the Kings. Any beginning reader would be able to figure this out just by reading. At the end of the Kings, we see the people going into captivity. With a little biblical history in my back pocket, I realized that the books of Daniel, Jeremiah, and Lamentations took place during this time of captivity, so I moved on to those books in my reading.

The same author, Luke, the physician, wrote the New Testament books of Luke and Acts. The gospel of Luke tells the story of Jesus from Luke's point of view, and Acts is a continuation of the story, telling of Jesus' ascension to heaven and the story of the early church. In the New Testament, you can also follow the train of thought of a given author in reading the writings of the apostle John or of Paul, for instance. John penned the gospel bearing his name, as well as 1, 2, and 3 John. He also wrote the prophetic book of Revelation, while Paul wrote most of the New Testament letters (sometimes called epistles), including Romans, 1 and 2 Corinthians, Galatians, Ephesians, Philippians, Colossians, 1 and 2 Thessalonians, 1 and 2 Timothy, Titus, and Philemon.

10. Accept grace.

As I mentioned earlier, I'm a recovering perfectionist. I hate messing up. I can't stand doing something wrong. It pains me to my bones to fall short of a goal that I've set. The goals I set as a perfectionist are always way too high. In other words, I have a very strong inborn tendency to beat myself up when I don't perform up to my own expectations. Now, I may outperform others, but that for me is not enough if I know I have not done my best. I can accept imperfection in others (well, usually), but learning to accept it in myself has been tough, and yet I am so fraught with imperfections.

So when you mess up and go for a week without reading, admit that you are human, ask God's forgiveness and help, and get back on the horse. Don't dwell on the mistakes and failures, look forward and bask in the love that God lavishes on you and move toward Him.

Our tendency when we aren't performing as we should is to shrink back, to stop trying, and to drift, at least that is my tendency. This is exactly what our adversary wants...for us to float through life, not making any waves at all. Instead, when we aren't on the top of our game, we need to draw near to God, knowing that He loves us warts and all. We need to accept that we are saved by grace and that we grow by grace (Galatians 3:3). We also need to accept that and that we will never be good enough on our own. It is all God.

11. Relax.

Enjoy the Word. Be diligent, yes. But don't be uptight. Don't set the clock; don't get the guilts and try to make it up if you miss a day. Find a comfortable spot to sit, put your feet up, and learn to enjoy spending time with your God. View your time in His Word as a time of rest and restoration. If reading through in a year is too fast for you, then find out what is comfortable and go for it.

12. Think of reading as a "get to do" instead of a "got to do."

At my children's school, those in charge are extremely security cautious and strictly limit the number of parents at each class party. In fact, with only four moms (or dads) per party, the only way a person has any chance of attending all parties is by being in charge—being the big Kahuna (or Head Room Mom, as they prefer to call it).

This past year was my first as the big Kahuna, and it was more than a little stressful since I am still learning what works and doesn't work with grade school children. On one particularly busy day of the week of the politically correct "Holiday Party," all of the last minute "stuff" seemed like such a burden. I was on my way to a cranky old day when I realized that "I don't have to do this, I get to do this." At that moment, my paradigm shifted dramatically. What an opportunity I had. How many others would have liked to do what I was getting to do but couldn't because of their work commitments and other encumbrances? How fortunate I was to have this fun opportunity with my son and his classmates! How fortunate are you to have a Bible and to be able to meet with God without fear of persecution!

13. Watch out for the trap of always "preparing" to start, always thinking about it and never doing it.

I like planning things to do, but sometimes the actual doing of them can get a little tough. Right now, you are preparing to start because you're reading this book. I hope that this will be of assistance to you, but don't get stuck here. Don't spend your Bible-reading time making a schedule to follow or reading commentaries about the Bible. Don't waste your time reading footnotes or general inspirational literature. Read the Bible. Jump in and go for it. Pray and move forward. As mentioned before, commentaries are great, and inspirational and devotional books can be a help, but they need to be in addition to the Bible, not in place of it. They are not God-breathed. The Bible is!

14. Track yourself in writing.

Have you ever been on a diet? Up until a few years ago, I never had been. I was always a skinny, athletic kid, but then I grew up and had children. Enough said.

Anyway, when it was finally time to drop a few pounds, I found that writing down what was going into my mouth was the best way to keep the right things going in and the wrong things out. If I don't journal when I diet, I don't lose weight. I have no way of benchmarking and assessing my progress. It is the same when reading your Bible, particularly when you're not reading sequentially. No matter how well you comprehend what you read, you're going to lose track of which of the sixty-six books you have and have not read if you're not writing it down. The easiest way to do this is to use your table of contents.

15. Use your table of contents.

We discussed this in an earlier section of the book, but just in case you're skimming, I want to make sure that you don't miss this point. A pencil and your table of contents are by far the simplest and, I think, best way to keep track of your reading. Don't worry about an elaborate schedule that you need to keep, boxes you need to check off, or a matrix the size of your wall to track yourself. Simply jot down your start date by your table of contents, pencil in the goal for completion (give yourself a year the first time through), and make sure that you read in the same Bible until you're done. This may sound silly, but you want to be able to read and record right away without any hassles. The lower the hassle factor, the higher the chance that you'll follow through. When I record books that I've read, I always do it in pencil so that I can erase my marks and use the same Bible for another read-through. Sometimes, I simply mark the books read with a simple check mark; other times through, I've dated the books by the month finished. The point here is that you have a simple, accessible way to track your progress so that you always know where you are.

Occasionally, I read more than one book concurrently as I rarely have what it takes to read straight through Isaiah, Ezekiel, or the Psalms. In cases where I am reading more than one book, I usually make a distinct mark next to the books I am currently reading, using just a dot to remind myself that I have begun a particular book. I then either keep a bookmark at the point I left off or simply mark my ending point with a pencil.

16. Experiment.

As you're learning to read your Bible, experiment a bit. Try reading at different times of day. Try different parts of the house. Read while you eat. Read without eating. Read in the chair, read in bed, read at the kitchen table. Read on your computer, read out of your regular Bible. Memorize. I can give you pointers, other people can give you tips, but in the end, you have to find what works for you and you won't figure out what's best if you haven't tried some different approaches.

17. Ask around for advice.

Don't be shy in asking others for advice. Chances are you know people who are serious students of God's Word. Ask what works for them and what doesn't. Allow yourself to be mentored or discipled by such people in your life. This isn't a sign of weakness...it's a sign of smarts. Really. Sure, as Westerners, we tend to think we can figure everything out by ourselves. You know there are tons of things we can figure out on our own, but why on earth should we stumble forward when we can stand on the shoulders of others and learn from both their successes and failures?

18. Do what works for you.

Go with what works for you. My husband can read at Caribou Coffee. The ambient noise there would drive me nuts. I, however, can read with the noise of kids in the background. Some people need the early morning time to read; some people need the late night. Really, what works for people varies. Figure out what works best for you and do it. This does not include the option of saying, "Nothing works for me." Some things will work better for you than others. Stick with it until you find your style and keep going.

19. Keep moving and don't give up.

Don't underestimate the importance of momentum. And whatever you do, don't punt. If you realize you can't make it through in a year, so what? Reassess your goals and keep moving. There's nothing magical about reading through the Bible in a year, but it is important to keep going and keep making progress.

When you're sitting still it's hard to get moving. Physics, my Dad tells me, tells us that a body in motion tends to stay in motion. The same thing is true here. Once you get moving, it's much easier to stay moving than to start, stop, and start again. Even if you have to move slowly, keep moving.

❦

Drawing Near

+ Set a mini-goal with a fun reward that you can meet this week.
+ Mark your beginning date of reading your Bible in the table of contents.
+ Consider what would be a reasonable amount of time for you to read through your Bible. Ask God if you should set this as a tentative goal.
+ Make a point to meet with Jesus every day this week but without a per day quota of chapters or verses (or books for you overachievers... yes, I know you're out there!).
+ Take two straight hours (or thirty minutes to an hour if the two-hour suggestion just gave you a facial tic) and read a chunk of Scripture of your choice.
+ Have coffee with at least one person you know who has a vital relationship with Jesus Christ and find out what challenges they have faced in reading the Word and what has worked well for them. Ask the person about the failures they have had in reading also.
+ If you wake up in the middle of the night, don't whine, sigh, or roll back over. Try getting up and spending some time with Jesus.

—6—

The Truth About Ability

God Loves the Underdog

THERE ARE A FEW WORDS that draw a response from me every time they are uttered in my house. One of the biggies is the phrase "I can't." "But Mom, I can't..." will always bring me out of my shell. Whenever one of my kids spouts up with an "I can't" statement, I chime in with, "Don't you mean, you have not yet been able to?" Sure, my son thinks it's an issue of semantics (even though he doesn't yet know what that word means), and you may too, but that doesn't change the fact that there is a world of difference between saying "I cannot" do something and "I have yet to do it." The first takes the pessimistic and easy way out. Failure accepted right from the beginning somehow hurts less since there is nothing invested.

The truth here, however, is that if you are reading this book, if you can read the newspaper or a magazine, you can read the Bible. Before the advent of more modern translations, understanding the phraseology was sometimes an issue, but with newer translations, the simple truth is if you can read you can read the Bible. Not only that, even if you're a terrible reader, if you can simply understand the spoken word, you can listen to the entire Bible on CD. There is no excuse for not ingesting the Word of God.

You know what else? As you start getting into the Bible for yourself, it becomes evident very quickly that God loves the underdog. He loves showing His great power in the face of human weakness. Seriously, what do you think are the odds of a ninety-year-old woman having a baby? Of city walls falling flat at the sound of a horn and a shout? Of 300 men conquering an entire army? Of a certain Person rising from the dead after three days in the grave? It is this same powerful God who wants to help you to know His Word and to set your heart ablaze with holy passion for Himself. Here are a few tips for surrendering and allowing His power to work in your life:

1. Pray!

I don't mean to be simplistic here, but praying and reading the Bible go together in more ways than just understanding what you're reading. One of the biggest keys I've found in having the desire for God's Word and the stamina to keep on moving is consistently praying for that desire. Do you think that it is God's will that His children desire His Word? Of course it is! And what does He promise about prayers asked in accordance with His will? He says that He will hear them and answer them (1 John 5:14–15).

God has a plan. When we align ourselves with that plan and pray in accordance with it, we will see results. It is like swimming downstream. I could pray tomorrow that God would drop a million bucks in small bills on my front porch. Does He have the power to do it? Sure. Will He? I can't imagine that He would, as this would not align with His purpose. However, if we pray for a desire for His Word, this does align with His Word and purpose in our lives. As followers of Christ, God's purpose is to transform us into the likeness of His Son, and His Word plays a huge part in this transformation.

If your desire for the Word has been quenched, pray. If necessary, pray and fast for that desire which you know is of God. Continue to pray that God would put a burning desire in your heart for His Word and His ways.

2. Get accountable.

There's nothing to give you a better initial kick in the pants to get going and keep going than answering to another person about what you have or have not been reading. This person needs to be someone who's close enough so that you can be honest when you don't measure up, but distant or respected enough so that you won't fall into the "lazy" routine. What, you ask, is the lazy routine? It goes something like this:

Week 1

Pam: Boy, I'm so excited about reading through the Bible this year! This is great isn't it?

Friend: Yeah, I'm just on fire! I read 1 Samuel this week, and next week I'm going to read the gospel of John!

Pam: Wow! That's great! This week I read Romans, and next week I'm going to get through Genesis and maybe start Exodus if I'm really on a roll!

Friend: Great! I'll see you next week.

Week 2

Pam: So, how'd this week go for you? It was a little tough on me.

Friend: It went okay, but not as well as I'd been hoping. Boy, I was just so tired, and the kids were just awful.

Pam: Yeah? Mine too.

Friend: So, it ends up I was going to read all of John, but I ended up only getting through the first three chapters.

Pam: Sounds like my week. I was reading in Genesis and only got up to Cain and Abel.

Friend: Oh well, it was a hard week. Some weeks are like that, right?

Pam: Oh absolutely. I had meetings two nights this week. My son had basketball practice. Then we had games all weekend. Oh, by the way, I can't meet next week. I'm in this drama at church.

Friend: That's all right. We'll just meet the following week. I'll keep going in John and you'll keep working in Genesis, right?

Pam: You got it. See you in two weeks.

Week 4

Pam: Things just seem to get busier and busier.

Friend: Here I thought it was just me. I have to be honest. I haven't read since the last time we met. I feel really bad about it, but there's just so much going on.

Pam: I have to tell you, you've just made me feel a lot better about myself! I haven't had a chance to read either. Life has just been so crazy.

Friend: You want to go for some coffee?

Pam: Yeah, sure, but I need to be home by 9:00...my show's on, you know! I never miss it!

Friend: Oh that's right, I've gotta get home too!

You get the point. The Bible says in Proverbs 27:17, "As iron sharpens iron, so one man sharpens another." But you know as well as I do that there are far more cardboard friends out there than iron ones. In the realm of accountability, it is critical not only to find but also to be an iron friend.

3. Accept the fact that reading the Bible is NOT rocket science.

God put the Bible in the language of the common man. The New Testament was not written in high style classical Greek, but in Koiné Greek, the common Greek language of the day. Jewish boys learned the Torah, the first five books of the Old Testament. The Word was and is accessible. The Bible was never intended to be a coffee table book that just sits there looking good or a shelf book that you have "just because every house needs one."

The simple fact is "The Bible is not rocket science!" We like to believe it is because in some way we feel that excuses us from the responsibility to live by its statutes. If we can't understand, we reason, how could God ever hold us to what is in it? But it is not rocket science. It is within our grasp. We need desperately to accept that fact and to bring that word to others.

4. Accept your weaknesses.

You are human. You are fallen. That's okay. Jesus loves fallen humans so much that He died for the whole lot of us. If you're thinking that you probably can't pull this one off by yourself, you're probably right. Stuart Smalley of *Saturday Night Live* fame might have you tell yourself, "I'm good enough, I'm smart enough, and doggone it, people like me," but I sure won't. Because you're not good enough without God. With Him, absolutely; without Him, you will more than likely fail. The beauty here is that the Bible tells us that God's power is perfected in our weakness (2 Corinthians 12:9). And that is where we need to focus, on the power that is at work within us, not on our own frailties!

5. When you run into the prophets, realize they speak the Words of God.

Here is a possible exception to the pencil rule we discussed earlier. If you think you can't read the Major Prophets, get a highlighter and start highlighting the words of God in the text. When you realize that these books are filled with God's specific words, it puts a different spin on it and makes it a lot easier to read…at least it did for me.

6. Realize who you are in Christ and what power is really at your disposal.

Have you ever read the New Testament book of Ephesians? Get this.
Ephesians 1:18–23, from the *God's Word* Translation:
> *I pray that the eyes of your heart may be enlightened, so that you will know what is the hope of His calling, what are the riches of the glory*

of His inheritance in the saints, and what is the surpassing greatness of His power toward us who believe. These are in accordance with the working of the strength of His might which He brought about in Christ, when He raised Him from the dead and seated Him at His right hand in the heavenly places, far above all rule and authority and power and dominion, and every name that is named, not only in this age but also in the one to come. And He put all things in subjection under His feet, and gave Him as head over all things to the church, which is His body, the fullness of Him who fills all in all.

Ephesians 1:18–23, from the GOD'S WORD Translation:
Then you will have deeper insight. You will know the confidence that he calls you to have and the glorious wealth that God's people will inherit. You will also know the unlimited greatness of his power as it works with might and strength for us, the believers. He worked with that same power in Christ when he brought him back to life and gave him the highest position in heaven. He is far above all rulers, authorities, powers, lords, and all other names that can be named, not only in this present world but also in the world to come. God has put everything under the control of Christ. He has made Christ the head of everything for the good of the church. The church is Christ's body and completes him as he fills everything in every way.

Can you even start to fathom everything that we have in Christ Jesus? It is like hitting the lottery, but much, much greater!

IN CHRIST JESUS:

- God has blessed us in the heavenly realms with every spiritual blessing in Christ.
- He chose us in Him before the creation of the world to be holy and blameless in His sight.
- He gives us His glorious grace in Christ.

- In Christ, we have redemption through His blood, the forgiveness of sins, in accordance with the riches of God's grace that He lavished on us with all wisdom and understanding.
- In Christ, we were chosen.
- In Christ, we hope.
- We were included in Christ when we heard the Word of truth.
- Having believed, we were marked in Christ with a seal, the promised Holy Spirit, who is a deposit guaranteeing our inheritance.
- We have His incomparably great power for us who believe. His power is like the working of His mighty strength, which He exerted in Christ when He raised Him from the dead and seated Him at His right hand in the heavenly realms, far above all rule and authority and power and dominion, and every title that can be given, not only in the present age but also in the one to come.
- God raised us up with Christ and seated us with Him in the heavenly realms in Christ Jesus, in order that in the coming ages he might show the incomparable riches of His grace, expressed in His kindness to us in Christ Jesus.
- We are God's workmanship, created in Christ Jesus to do good works, which God prepared in advance for us to do.
- In Christ, we who were far away have been brought near through the blood of Christ.
- In Christ, we are being built together...
- We are sharers together in the promise in Christ Jesus.
- God's eternal purpose was accomplished in Christ Jesus.
- In Christ and through faith in Him, we may approach God with freedom and confidence.
- Truth is in Christ Jesus.
- In Christ, God forgave us.

What kind of power does the follower of Christ have according to Ephesians? The same mighty power that raised Christ from the dead! That's power! And if you belong to Christ, that is the power that He uses in your life. It doesn't matter how weak you think you are...that kind of power is enough for anybody!

7. Explore the spiritual disciplines.

The spiritual disciplines have largely been lost by today's evangelical culture. Nonetheless, they are invaluable as aides to spiritual growth and formation. Realize that these are not ends in themselves, but merely tools to use along the spiritual journey.

The disciplines are generally grouped differently by different authors, for example, Richard Foster, *Celebration of Discipline*, looks at them as Inward, Outward, and Corporate:

- *Inward:* Meditation, Prayer, Fasting, and Study
- *Outward:* Simplicity, Solitude, Submission, and Service
- *Corporate:* Confession, Worship, Guidance, and Celebration[4]

Dallas Willard, *The Spirit of the Disciplines*, looks at them as Disciplines of Abstinence and Engagement:

- *Disciplines of Abstinence:* Solitude, Silence, Fasting, Frugality, Chastity, Secrecy, and Sacrifice
- *Disciplines of Engagement:* Study, Worship, Celebration, Service, Prayer, Fellowship, Confession, and Submission[5]

For a full discussion on the disciplines, you'll need to check out either Foster or Willard as that lies well beyond the scope of this book. However, let me quickly note that solitude with God will change your life. When you try fasting, you'll realize that it is not just for an age gone by. And simple living with less stuff translates into more time. Don't believe it? Try it and see for yourself.

8. Start a group.

While the accountability of another individual works best for some people, others may find the support and encouragement they need in a group. Consider forming a group to read through the Bible together over the course of a year or two. When I say "read together," I'm not talking about reading the same material at the same pace, but rather having a group that meets once a month or so to share with one another where each person has been reading and how things are going. Hopefully, you'll have at least one or two strong people in the group who can encourage and exhort the weaker members to continue on and finish.

Another up side to meeting as a group is that when you begin sharing with each other where you are reading and how it is going, you will be alerted to difficult areas, as well as really good books, through the experience of others in the group. When you see another of flesh and blood actually succeed and make it through Leviticus or Isaiah, then you'll gain that extra measure of encouragement to know that you can make it, too!

9. Enlist someone to pray for you in your mission.

Sure, you'll feel stupid if you ask someone to pray for you and then you fail. But guess what! The odds that you will fail go down dramatically if you seek out a prayer warrior to help you on your mission. I'm not talking here about just asking your best friend to pray for you, not unless that person is a true prayer warrior. Be watchful of the people in your church; find out who has the gift of intercession. Ask God to lead you to the right person or people to pray for you, and ask them to help pray you through your mission. When you run into tough times, call them with specific prayer requests. When you have success, let them rejoice with you.

10. Talk about what you read.

Okay. This is going to seem a little weird at first, especially if you hang out with people who are biblically illiterate. However, talking with someone about what you are reading helps you not only process what you are taking in, but it helps connect the Bible to your daily life. When you verbalize what you read, you begin to interact with it on another level because to be able to talk about something you've read means you must have read with a degree of comprehension. You can't just rip through five pages, make a check mark in a box, and be on your way. To talk about something intelligently, you need to be a careful reader. You need to be interacting with the text, looking for the point, trying to understand. All of a sudden, relevance increases, if from nothing more than the fact that it has become a center of discussion in your real-life conversations.

Additionally, when something comes out of your own mouth, you will tend to have more "buy in" to the application. Several years ago, my husband and I participated in a parenting class. One of the points stressed in helping children to obey was to call for a verbal response. For instance, when I ask my son to come to the dinner table, it is his job to answer with an affirmative, "Yes, Mom." Similarly, if I am giving instructions to a smaller member of the family, I will ask the child to repeat back to me what they are going to do. In that repeating back of the information, they not only remind themselves of the instructions, but by verbalizing it with their little mouths, they have a higher degree of "buy in." Does it always work? No, but it certainly does help.

11. Take someone else along for the ride.

Once you get on a roll and start making progress in your Bible reading, take someone else along for the ride. Now, you may already have a partner or a group that you're reading with. That's fine. Find others to join you on the way. As you begin to see success in your reading, share that excitement with others and encourage them. There will doubtless come a time in your spiritual life when you'll need someone to come along and give you encouragement. So while you're rolling, don't be selfish, but instead reach out and lovingly spur others on and encourage them in their walks!

12. Anticipate and prepare for opposition.

Satan doesn't want you reading the Bible. I don't know how to say it more simply. Cut off from the Word of God, you are spiritually impotent. Do nothing and you are of no real concern to the adversary; you're actually playing on his team. But get yourself into the Word of God and you become an armed soldier. Does this mean we should let a sleeping dog lie, so to speak, and stay away from the Word? Of course not! But do realize that while the difficulty for us in reading the Word of God may seem like it is mainly in issues of time or worldly things, the battles we fight in life are truly of a spiritual nature. In Ephesians 6:12, Paul tells us, "our struggle is not against flesh and blood, but against the rulers, against the powers, against the world forces of this darkness, against the spiritual forces of wickedness in the heavenly places." It is for this reason that he goes on to tell us to arm ourselves with the full armor of God.

13. Put on the full armor of God.

Truth be told, when you start swinging the sword of the Spirit, it becomes evident to all that you are part of the active battle. The Word is the one offensive weapon we have on the battlefield (although it, too, is used defensively at times). Paul tells us about the equipment that we need to deal with as soldiers on this spiritual battlefield in Ephesians 6:13–17:

> *Therefore, take up the full armor of God, so that you will be able to resist in the evil day, and having done everything, to stand firm. Stand firm therefore, having girded your loins with truth, and having put on the breastplate of righteousness, and having shod your feet with the preparation of the gospel of peace; in addition to all, taking up the shield of faith with which you will be able to extinguish all the flaming arrows of the evil one. And take the helmet of salvation, and the sword of the Spirit, which is the word of God.*

Although all analogies fall short at certain points, think for a moment with me of a football game. Eleven players from each side stand between the lines at any given point. More guys are members of the team, to be sure, but spend a good portion of the game sitting on the bench or roaming the sidelines. They're wearing their snazzy shirts and cute little pants, but as long as they're outside of the lines and not engaging the other team in battle, they really don't have to worry about getting clocked! Of course, they're not helping their own team either when they're outside the lines. Anyone knowing an ounce about sports will understand the point here, OFFENSE DRAWS OPPOSITION. So when you pick up a weapon of offense spiritually, you must be wearing your defensive armor. A running back on a football team would never think of carrying the ball without wearing his helmet and other protective gear. Neither should you.

14. Decide even before you start that you will pursue God the hardest when you feel least like doing it.
You need to understand right up front that while reading through the Bible is totally within your grasp, it will not be easy sailing the whole way. Days will come when you feel distant from God. You may know why. You may not. You may be bored or tired or angry or frustrated or depressed. God may seem distant. Seek God in these times. Go to the Gospels, look at your Savior, and press on diligently as the author of Hebrews would exhort. When you feel most like pulling away, press in to God. Draw near to the throne of grace. The author of Hebrews puts it so eloquently, explaining that in Jesus, we have a merciful high priest who can sympathize with us because He too was a man:

> For we do not have a high priest who cannot sympathize with our weaknesses, but One who has been tempted in all things as we are, yet without sin. "Therefore, let us draw near with confidence to the throne of grace, so that we may receive mercy and find grace to help in time of need." (Hebrews 4:15–16)

15. Pursue God especially when you feel most distant and least worthy.

Ever make a big mistake? We all do. Maybe it was a moral slip-up. Maybe your mouth got the better of you. Maybe a bitter spirit has a grip over you. Maybe you just feel cheesed, and you're not even sure why. Ever just feel distant? Whatever the case, when we fail God, we often just feel like avoiding Him. We feel like we are not worthy. Of course, apart from Christ, we aren't worthy. God knows our failures. Jesus understands our trials and temptations. He can sympathize. We need desperately to learn the four main exhortations of the book of Hebrews.

16. Learn the four exhortations of Hebrews: Consider Jesus, Hold Fast, Draw Near, Press On.

Consider Jesus: Hebrews 3:1 — "Therefore, holy brethren, partakers of a heavenly calling, **consider Jesus**, the Apostle and High Priest of our confession" (boldface mine).

Hold Fast: Hebrews 3:6 — "But Christ was faithful as a Son over His house—whose house we are, if we **hold fast** our confidence and the boast of our hope firm until the end" (boldface mine).

Hebrews 3:14 — "For we have become partakers of Christ, if we **hold fast** the beginning of our assurance firm until the end..." (boldface mine).

Draw Near: Hebrews 4:16 — "Therefore let us **draw near** with confidence to the throne of grace, so that we may receive mercy and find grace to help in time of need" (boldface mine).

Press On: Hebrews 6:1 — "Therefore leaving the elementary teaching about the Christ, let us **press on** to maturity" (boldface mine).

17. Pray some more!

Keep praying. Keep praying for the continued desire to read. Keep praying that God will open your eyes as you read to give you eyes that see and ears that hear. Pray every time you read. Prayer is key, and yet it can be so easy to forget, especially if you are having success. When we get firing on all cylinders with God, it can be easy to forget what a gift it all is. Salvation is a gift; the faith to believe is a gift; the desire to read is a gift. None of it is of you. It is all of Him. Certainly, we respond, but we need always to remember the source and to continue diligently in prayer as we grow.

18. Stop being afraid of the Bible.

Now if you're in the faint of heart category, which I sometimes (okay a lot of the times) am myself, you may be thinking, "Okay, if offense draws opposition, maybe I should just sit here on the sidelines. And after all, the Bible is a really long book, and I probably wouldn't be able to finish it anyway, and if I did, what are the chances I'd be able to understand it?"

Let's be honest here, many adults are just plain afraid of the Bible. They're afraid they won't understand, or they're afraid of the changes that they'll have to make if they do understand. I often wonder where in life it is that we pick up this pessimistic outlook. It must, however, be somewhere after the second grade.

Not long ago, while teaching a first and second grade Sunday school class, I explained to the kids that I was going to read the story right out of the Bible to show them they could understand it right from the source, without me having to explain it or read it from a "kid Bible." I told them that I wanted to do this because many grown-ups think that the Bible is too hard to understand, but that I wanted them to grow up knowing the truth—they can understand the Bible. They looked back at me incredulous! Grown-ups thinking the Bible is hard to understand? I must be kidding! I went on to read to them right out of the *New Living Translation* of the Bible, having to clarify only a couple of phrases along the way, and they answered all the questions I had for them. Too hard? No way, not with the right translation!

19. Find the right translation!

We talked about it in the previous chapter, but the importance of this point begs another mention. Reading a translation that you can understand can make the difference between success and failure. If I had to venture a guess as to why many in the over-thirty crowd think that reading through the Bible is just too hard, it would have to be that we were weaned on the *King James Version* of the Bible. Not that there's anything terribly wrong with that version, particularly if you lived in the 1600s. We just don't talk the way that version was translated. Fortunately for us, we have several excellent translations to choose from today. As mentioned earlier, I highly recommend the *New Living Translation* or the *GOD'S WORD Translation* for first-time readers. The *New International Version* is also a very readable Bible. As we talked about in the last chapter, the *New American Standard Bible* remains the standard for Bible study, because of its word for word translation from the Greek text, but it can be harder when simply reading for general context. Eventually, do read through the *New American Standard*...it's still my favorite for study...just don't start there.

20. Don't worry that you're inadequate or not smart enough.

I wish that each person reading this book could meet a friend of mine. Her name is Michelle. She is one of my heroes. I first met Michelle several years ago when she was in her late teens. She is now twenty five years old. Michelle is a special young lady. She has some learning disabilities. She doesn't drive. She works as an assistant activities coordinator at a long-term care facility. To speak casually with Michelle, you would never be able to guess what a student of the Bible she is. In fact, at age twenty-two, she has already read through the entire Bible in a year—several years earlier in her life than I did in mine! She has also attended a Precept Bible Study class (an in-depth study on Hebrews) for the past two years. For those not familiar with Precept studies, the studies require approximately five hours of homework each week in preparation for class time. As I was chatting with Michelle the other night, she informed me that she had spent her afternoon on Sunday typing the rest of her class notes into her word processor. I was blown away. Like I said, she can't drive, but God has given Michelle the desire for His Word, and the degree of understanding that she needs. If each of us did with what we have what Michelle does with what she has, I'm convinced God would use us to turn the world upside down!

21. Realize that it is God who is doing the work in you.

In other words, don't even think about getting full of yourself. The book of Proverbs counsels that, "Pride goes before destruction, and a haughty spirit before stumbling." As we make progress in reading through the Word, God will use it to change us from the inside out. The sin nature, however, still rears its head on occasion and tries to persuade us that we have made such spiritual progress because of our own hard work and superior skills. Baloney! It is by the grace of God that we are saved, and it is by the grace of God that we have the power to persevere. Remember, once you've started looking at how cool you think you are, you've taken your eyes off of the goal, off of Jesus, and you're headed for trouble.

22. Focus on your mission; look to the goal, not to the obstacles.

Why do we spend so much more time looking at the obstacles instead of focusing on the goal? It's too hard, it's too long. I don't have the time. Stop it. Look to the goal of Jesus. When a runner competes in a race, he must fix his eyes on the goal. We must fix our eyes on Jesus as the author of Hebrews exhorts.

23. Move forward based on your faith and not your feelings.

I speak here to myself as much as anyone. Women especially need to hear this one. We are creatures of feelings. This is fine when we're talking about chick flicks and the like, but when we get to issues of faith, we can't let ourselves run on feelings or the adversary will deceive us every time. Satan is more powerful than you are on your own. No comparison. He is the father of lies and the schemes that he uses he uses on our minds. If he can use your feelings to deceive you, do you think he will? Absolutely. He doesn't play fair. That is why you need to know the full counsel of God. He does. And he'll twist it to suit his purpose in deceiving you every time if you let him.

Let's try this one on for size: Have you ever feared that you have committed the unpardonable sin that Jesus talks about, blasphemy against the Holy Spirit or that you are the man of Hebrews 6, the one of whom the writer says, "It is impossible to renew them again to repentance." You don't have to be a Bible teacher very long before one of these issues pops up. It is a common scheme of Satan to make believers doubt their salvation. (Just for the record, biblical scholars overwhelmingly agree that if you're afraid that you've committed one of these sins, you haven't because if you had you wouldn't care!) These verses can be terrifying if taken out of the context of the whole. Whenever I have a scared student on my hands, I send them to the book of John, specifically chapter ten that clearly teaches that of all that the Father has given to the Son, He will lose none. If this isn't assurance, I don't know what is.

Still, there are times we will not feel saved. We will be under attack. Guess what? If you're under attack, it is an evidence of the reality of the spiritual world. Our job? We are to stand firm in the faith. (See 1 Peter 5:9.) God has not given us a spirit of fear, but one of power, and of love, and of a sound mind. (See 2 Timothy 1:7.) He has given us weapons of warfare: defensive weapons and an offensive one, the sword of the Spirit, which is the Word of God.

24. Meet with Jesus every day!

I had a theology professor in college who advised our class that no matter where we were reading in our Bibles, each one of us should meet with Jesus every day. Read even a few sentences from the Gospels when you're reading elsewhere in the Bible just to make sure that you are looking on the face of your Savior and Lord everyday. Do I always do this? No. I can tell you, though, that when the world is beating me down, and I need strength for my soul (and I'm thinking clearly enough), I run to the

Gospels because there is nothing like looking on the face of Jesus to quicken your spirit!

25. Realize that God looks for people with whole hearts to strongly support.

As I close with my practical points, I'd like to leave you with some of the most encouraging words that I've found in the Bible. This may surprise you, but they come from the book of 2 Chronicles 16:9a: "For the eyes of the LORD move to and fro throughout the earth that He may strongly support those whose heart is completely His."

Drawing Near

- Identify the lies that you've been holding in regard to reading your Bible.

- Spend some time praying and asking God to guide you in your prayer life.

- Read the letter to the Ephesians, circle every occurrence of the phrase "in Christ," and then make a list and find out what you learn from each occurrence.

- Read one of the Gospels and observe the need of Jesus to spend time with His heavenly Father. See how often He withdrew from the crowds for solitude with God. Then consider this question: If Jesus, being fully God in a human body, sinless and the whole nine-yards, needed solitude with the Father regularly, how can I ever think that I can function without that myself? What would be the root of thinking that suggests that I have no time for solitude with God?

- When you experience a time of opposition this week (too tired, too busy, too bored, feelings of unworthiness, and the list goes on) resolve to press into God through reading His Word, even if it is only for a short time.

- Memorize 2 Chronicles 16:9a.

- Read the book of James, and seek God's leading in finding a prayer warrior.

- Read in the Proverbs to find out what God has to say about wisdom and seek His leading in finding a wise accountability partner.

- Just in case you missed the opportunity last week, here it is again… Make a point to meet with Jesus somewhere in the Gospels every day.

Part 2

Carrying
the Fire

GOD'S POWER IN THE
TRANSFORMED LIFE

As we have seen, the goal of being in the Word of God, of reading the Bible, is not simple head knowledge. The whole point of being in God's Word is coming to know the God of the Word in an intimate relationship. It is in this intimate relationship that holy passion is unleashed and fanned into flame. God has revealed Himself through His Word, and it is primarily through His Word that He transforms us and changes us from the inside out. As we abide in His Word and the Word richly dwells in us and transforms us, we become people of the Word whose passion begins to impact and infect those around us. Fire, you see, has a way of spreading.

THE PROBLEM OF CULTURE

Have you ever noticed, though, that the sinful culture in which we live has turned us into such an egocentric bunch that most of us in the church think spiritually in the realm of individualism? We want more spiritual passion, but we are so culturally accustomed to thinking only of ourselves that we open ourselves up to a very compelling lie from the enemy. It is at this point that Satan often kicks in a very subtle, very destructive lie truly disguised as an angel of light. The lie goes something like this: "Getting spiritual passion is going to take too much time. It is going to take time away from your spouse and kids. It is going to take time away from the work you do which is so important to your family. Goodness, it is even going to take time away from the work you do for God! And for what? So you can feel good spiritually? And hey, you may put all that time in and find out it doesn't even work? You are so selfish! Or stupid! Or maybe it's both...yeah, selfish and stupid. Spiritual passion is for other people who are more spiritual and who have more time on their hands. It certainly isn't for you!"

But you see, spiritual passion is not just something for you! Don't you see? We are on a mission from God! We'll get back to this concept later, but for now, suffice it to say that the pursuit of God is the least selfish and most wise investment of time you can make. Don't let the enemy tell you otherwise. You can be a passionate carrier of the infectious Word, one who reflects the light of Jesus to your world, or you can be a barrier to the Word, one who professes Christ, but lives for self and thereby serves as a hindrance to the kingdom.

Are both true Christians? Good question! We'll examine that a little closer later on. For now, let's consider life change that comes as God Himself ignites spiritual passion within us.

—7—
Carriers or Barriers?

I HAVE A COUPLE OF BIG DOGS. REALLY BIG DOGS. They're Great Danes who, given the height of their cropped ears, are nearly as tall as my seven-year-old daughter...and they outweigh her by a lot! (With a little dieting and exercise on my part, one day the pups should outweigh me!) One of my kids' favorite outings is to take Abby and Angel over to the local Petsmart store to browse and shop. Let's just say that when we arrive at the store, we're not exactly flying under the radar. In fact, as I write this, they are only six-month old puppies, but their combined weight is nearly 200 pounds. They are almost always the biggest dogs at Petsmart unless we run into an adult Dane. However, their taped ears give people the signal that, "Yes, in spite of our size we are puppies." They also have that characteristic non-coordination seen primarily in large breed puppies and teenage boys. There are times they literally don't know what to do with their limbs. (This poses some extreme problems on the stairs from time to time.) But they always know what to do around people...greet them with enthusiasm!

My pups are literally smile carriers. Take them to Petsmart, and you'll see more grins than in a house of twenty kids on Christmas morning. They're not doing anything exceptionally special or out of the ordinary; they're just being who they are as God's creation. They are smile carriers.

Now, of course, the people who frequent Petsmart are predisposed to smiling when they see dogs of this kind, but don't miss the point: These dogs are carrying something that is affecting people positively. Everywhere they walk, they bring something positive. Everyone and everything that comes in contact with them is touched for the good, albeit in a small way.

If smiles were contagious, you could catch one by running into either of these pups. In our house, we affectionately refer to them as our "smile carriers." When we are in relationship with Jesus, and are abiding in His Word, something happens to us. Better yet, something happens inside of us that changes us. It is clear throughout the Bible that you can't know God and remain who you were. In fact, when the Holy Spirit takes up residence in us and we walk in the Spirit, we become carriers of the love of God who point others to the One who indwells us.

Paul puts it this way in his letter to the church at Galatia saying, "I have been crucified with Christ, nevertheless I live, yet not I, but Christ lives in me and the life I live in the flesh I live by faith in the Son of God who loved me and gave Himself over on my behalf" (Galatians 2:20, my translation). We have come a long way in our journey of getting to know God through His written Word. Knowing His Word is vitally important and is so neglected in our day. However, as we learn to read the Bible and take it in, we need always to be mindful of the fact that God never intended for us to absorb Bible knowledge and keep it safely locked up and cataloged in our heads. Yet how often do we see this happening? More often than we should. As a Bible teacher, I constantly run up against people who like to bring this up. It usually goes something like this, "Well, I know that the Bible is important, but I just see these ladies who have been in the same study year and after year, and I don't see it having any effect on their lives. It seems like it's all head knowledge to me."

Well, head knowledge of the Bible is important in following Jesus; it just is. The Bible is the very Word of God, and head knowledge of God's Word is important because His Word is truth. You see, even if you assent to the fact that the Bible is totally true, and that it is the only true guide for life, if you don't know what is in it, your belief in its veracity is essentially worthless. You can't live by principles you don't know. You'll never be a person of the Word if you're not in the Word. Head knowledge isn't a problem unless the knowledge is only in the head. The "head knowledge" problem happens when the truth fails to permeate our lives, when knowledge is loved for the sake of itself instead of as the truth that causes us to walk more and more in conformity with Jesus by the power of the indwelling Holy Spirit.

You see, the more you walk with Jesus in prayer and His Word, the more your life should be, well, shiny. In other words, the closer you grow to Jesus through His Word, the more your life will shine to others as Jesus describes in His famous words from the Sermon on the Mount in Matthew 5:16: "Let your light shine before men that they may see your good works and glorify your Father who is in heaven."

In the back of this book, you'll find a Bible study tool box with a short inductive Bible study that looks at a few shiny people from Scripture, people of exceptional spiritual passion who will help us understand what the life transformed by the Word of God looks like. First, however, we need to ask some serious questions about why the church as a whole has dullness about it in our day. Why is it that we often see more "barrier" Christians than "carrier" Christians?

Let's face it: The church of Jesus Christ should be a very shiny place. We are called to let our light shine, to be as a city set on a hill, a lamp on a stand. Maybe things are different where you live, but there are many claiming the name of Jesus who are anything but shiny, people who may want heaven and a place to hang out on Sunday mornings but who want nothing of the Word of God or the life of a disciple.

Much (dare I say most?) of those professing to be believers today do not know the Word of God. Yes, there are some who drink in the Word, who meditate on God's precepts, and who study to show themselves approved unto God as Paul speaks of in his letter to Timothy. But do the wholehearted believers make up the majority of people who show up on Sundays?

While we would never mouth the words, when we ignore the Word of God we say with our very lives, "I don't need God. I can do it better myself. My time is best spent somewhere else." I know this is unpleasant to hear, but is it not truth, my friend? With our computers and palm pilots and our e-mail and wireless, we have forgotten the only connection that we really need is the connection with our Creator through His revealed Word.

The logical question, then, becomes, "Why are we as a group biblically illiterate and what can be done about it?"

Consider the parable of the Sower of the Seed from Luke 8:4-18:

> When a large crowd was coming together, and those from the various cities were journeying to Him, He spoke by way of a parable: "The sower went out to sow his seed; and as he sowed, some fell beside the road, and it was trampled under foot and the birds of the air ate it up. Other [seed] fell on rocky [soil], and as soon as it grew up, it withered away, because it had no moisture. Other [seed] fell among the thorns; and the thorns grew up with it and choked it out. Other [seed] fell into the good soil, and grew up, and produced a crop a hundred times as great." As He said these things, He would call out, "He who has ears to hear, let him hear."
>
> His disciples [began] questioning Him as to what this parable meant. And He said, "To you it has been granted to know the mysteries of the kingdom of God, but to the rest [it is] in parables, so that "seeing they may not see, and hearing they may not understand."
>
> "Now the parable is this: the seed is the word of God. Those beside the road are those who have heard; then the devil comes and takes away the word from their heart, so that they will not believe and be saved. Those on the rocky [soil] are those who, when they hear, receive the word with joy; and these have no [firm] root; they believe for a while, and in time of temptation fall away. The [seed] which fell

among the thorns, these are the ones who have heard, and as they go on their way they are choked with worries and riches and pleasures of [this] life, and bring no fruit to maturity. But the [seed] in the good soil, these are the ones who have heard the word in an honest and good heart, and hold it fast, and bear fruit with perseverance.

"Now no one after lighting a lamp covers it over with a container, or puts it under a bed; but he puts it on a lampstand, so that those who come in may see the light. For nothing is hidden that will not become evident, nor [anything] secret that will not be known and come to light. So take care how you listen; for whoever has, to him [more] shall be given; and whoever does not have, even what he thinks he has shall be taken away from him."

Before we move forward, let me give you a word of encouragement. The very fact that you are reading a book to learn how to read the Bible for yourself says a lot about you. It says that you desire to read the Word and that you're seeking to follow God. You may not have been successful in the past, but the reading of this book shows a heart at least bent in the right direction. I say this here because the words that follow may seem harsh to those souls of sensitive conscience. However, I fear not saying them because we live in the age of the seared conscience, the age of tolerance, and political correctness where nothing is wrong and everyone is "okay."

In light of this parable, though, I would propose that everyone is not okay. Jesus interprets the parable for us, telling us what kind of person each type of soil represents. Let's look for a moment, by way of application, at some of the general categories of and reasons for biblical illiteracy. Considering the four types of soil, we can make reasonable application to the following four types of biblically illiterate people we see in the church today.

JUST TAKING UP SPACE

These folks are the seed along the path. Okay, so it doesn't sound too politically correct, but some churchgoers simply take up space. They attend in order to see and be seen. Maybe they're looking for the networking potential or like the sound of "church member" on a resume. They come to please spouses or parents. Some have "always" come and just keep coming. Nothing gets through to them; they're annoyed when the pastor preaches one minute over his allotted time. Noon kick-off is infinitely more important than worship of the true and living God. They take up space and nothing more. They are not saved and make no claim to be. They are simply "there." Unfortunately, people in this category often become hardened and immune to the gospel message. They continue to reject both the gospel and the Author of salvation. They're biblically illiterate because at the end of the day, they simply don't care.

THE EASY BELIEVERS

Easy believers are represented in the parable by the seed on the rocky soil. While these individuals may show up on Sundays, many visit just once or twice every few years. They've bought a nonbiblical salvation, a fire insurance that sounded great at the time of sale. It's all about "asking Jesus into your heart" and going about business as usual. It's assenting to a set of facts and living just as if you've always lived. This group only has part of the story because they only really want part of the story. They want what Dietrich Bonhoeffer calls cheap grace:

> Cheap grace is the deadly enemy of our Church...Cheap grace means the justification of the sin without the justification of the sinner...Cheap grace is the preaching of forgiveness without requiring repentance, baptism without church discipline, Communion without confession, absolution without personal confession. Cheap grace is grace without discipleship, grace without the cross, grace without Jesus Christ, living and incarnate.[6]

Tragically, in response to the social gospel of the early twentieth century, which presented a nonbiblical, works-based salvation, Christianity in the late twentieth century overreacted toward an easy-believism. The church today still suffers the results of this swing as seen in the biblically illiterate who believe that they have been saved by a recitation of words, almost an "incantation" of sorts, as opposed to a relationship with Jesus. They often make a profession and then just as quickly as they were "saved" vanish from the scene. The easy believers are illiterate because they think that salvation is fire insurance, and theirs has been bought and paid for. They hear only that which tickles their ears and otherwise refuse to be burdened with the Word.

THE ENCUMBERED

The encumbered are represented by the seed on the thorny soil, and they are quite possibly the saddest lot of all. They hear the Word, they know it's true, but the "stuff" of life gets in the way. They are too busy to study the Word. They can't find the time in the midst of their jobs, investments, worries, mortgage payments, boats, and cars. Could it be, too, that some also cannot find the time in the midst of their ministries and "doings" for God? A big God who desires a relationship and obedience simply does not fit into the crowded lives of those who are encumbered. The encumbered are biblically illiterate because they will not, and eventually cannot, shed the encumbrances to make time to mature.

THE IMMATURE

The immature are like the seed on the good soil that had not yet grown. Many in our churches are biblically illiterate because they are babes or small children in Christ. My friend, because you have chosen to read this book, my guess is that you fall somewhere in this category, somewhere along the continuum between newborn Christian and the maturity the author of Hebrews calls us to press toward. I'm on the continuum, too. I certainly have not yet arrived, but I am pressing on, and my heart is that you will, too.

When my daughter was three, she couldn't read a lick, but I knew she would soon because she desired to learn. She so wished she could pick up a book like her older brother and read. In fact, she often made up her own stories that matched the pictures in her books in order to move in the direction of reading. I was not downtrodden that Kate couldn't read. I read to her and encouraged her growth, knowing that with proper nurture she would inevitably grow mentally and be able to read, just as she continues to grow physically. Children mature. Babies grow up. That's just the way life is. And that's just the way spiritual life is as well. We are born as babes. Although enlightened by the Holy Spirit to understand the truth of the gospel, spiritual babes often arrive biblically illiterate unless they happen to have had some church background prior to regeneration.

Is there anything wrong with being a baby? No way! Babies are cute and lovable. They need to be cared for and nurtured. Nothing wrong with being a baby either physically or spiritually. Immaturity is not a problem if it is only a stage through which one is passing.

Some in our churches today are simply baby Christians and are biblically illiterate because they have not yet learned what they will as they mature in Christ and read His Word. They're starting to learn, they just haven't quite arrived yet. They will, however, grow and bring forth a crop, because all who are truly saved bear fruit. Not all bear the same amount, but all bear fruit.

ASKING THE TOUGH QUESTION

Your hang-ups in trying to read the Bible may very well be due to spiritual immaturity. You may be an infant in Christ who simply has never been taught some of the basics of getting into the Word of God, or you may have other issues linked to this immaturity, such as simple problems of discipline, like a person who finds it hard to get up in the morning, to go running, or to put down the doughnut or bag of chips.

It's possible, however, that you have been in the church for a length of time without ever interacting with the Bible. Now you're reading this book not because you desire the Word, but you just think that reading is the right thing to do. If this is the case, then your problems with the Bible may go deeper to more core issues of what it means to be a Christian. Don't shut me down here. If you find yourself disagreeing, make a note of it in the margin and resolve to examine the concept as you read through the Bible for yourself.

We know from hearing the words of Jesus that many who listened to Him simply did not "get it." He described them as having ears, but not hearing—as having eyes, but not seeing. Throughout the Bible, we encounter people who try outwardly to look like they are following God, but whose hearts are far from Him. They encounter the Word of God, but for whatever reason, it does not take root and bear fruit.

I remember my college days when I had to read certain scholarly books on the Bible written by men whose names were followed by a veritable alphabet of credentials. They knew more about the Bible than you could ever imagine, but they did not know Jesus. To them, the Bible proved academically challenging, but spiritually, they could not open its pages because they did not have eyes to see or ears to hear. They didn't know Jesus. To them, He was an interesting human being, but they could not grasp Him as divine. The Gospels were not God-breathed, in their opinion, but were merely the result of many different editors, or redactors as they called them, who added and changed and essentially made up most of the gospel story.

Reading the works of such academics tears my heart because it is obvious that after spending an entire lifetime pursuing knowledge of the Bible they themselves are on their way to a Christless eternity. Understand here, that this is not an attack on biblical scholarship. Biblical scholarship, done by men and women who know Jesus as their Lord and Savior, is a treasure to the church. Biblical scholarship apart from a relationship with the Author, however, is pointless.

So, you're asking, how do these people relate to me? Here are some questions for you to consider:

Is it possible to interact with the things of God without knowing God?

Is it possible to be a member of the visible church without being part of the body?

Quite honestly, we could debate our theories all day, but the only place where the true answers lie is in the Word of God. Jesus says that there are those who will cry out to Him, "Lord, Lord," and will not enter the kingdom of heaven. That being the case, can we ever know that we are saved? Absolutely. Can we be deceived by our enemy into thinking we are saved, when we are not? You bet. If this were not so, there would be no call in the Bible to examine ourselves to see if we are, in fact, in Christ Jesus. The apostle John would not have had to write his first epistle to explain how we can know that we have eternal life.

The gospel of John clearly tells us that if we belong to Christ He will not lose us, for no one can snatch us out of His hand. The question, then, I believe, is not if we can lose what we have, but have we ever had it in the first place? And knowing God in a saving manner is the basis for any meaningful interaction with Scripture.

How to Know if You Know Him

So, can you be sure that you really know Him? Can you know for sure if you are the seed that has a true root? If you study for yourself, I believe you will come to the conclusion that the Bible not only calls us to examine our own lives to see if we are truly saved, but it gives us some very clear guidelines for such a spiritual examination. The whole point of the book of 1 John is that its readers might know that they have eternal life, as John says in the conclusion to this letter: "These things I have written to you who believe in the name of the Son of God, so that you may know that you have eternal life" (1 John 5:13).

Now before you start the "Drawing Near" section this week, you need to understand something. The questions may sound a little simplistic or even judgmental, but they are not my questions, they are God's. As much as we'd like to pin our salvation on a simple altar call and prayer, the Bible maintains throughout that true belief results in changed lives.

In a nutshell, then, if you have never experienced growth in your spiritual life, if God is only a weekend acquaintance, if you live in continual bondage under sin (anger, bitterness, addictions, sexual issues, you name it), if you just can't stand the people at church, if you're being crushed under the weight of this world, and if you just can't seem to experience a victory, maybe—just maybe, the reason your Bible is a closed book to you is that you have never been truly saved, and only those who have truly been ignited by the Spirit can burn with passion for God.

If after reading 1 John you think you may fall into this category, it's time to put down this book, pick up your Bible and read through the gospel of John and then the book of Romans.

Drawing Near

Take a few minutes to read through the book of 1 John and ask yourself the following questions:

1. Do I have fellowship with the Father?
2. Am I abiding in Him?
3. Am I practicing sin habitually?
4. Do I have God's love?
5. Do I love the brethren?
6. Am I overcoming?

Ablaze

—8—

Carriers on a Mission from God

DO YOU WAKE UP in the morning as a person on a mission? If so, what is your mission? Is it to make as much money as possible and dominate in your job? Maybe you wake up with the mission of just getting through the day and surviving your toddlers (been there!). Maybe it's a community service project that's really close to your heart or some special ministry you have at the church. Or maybe you just roll out of bed because that's what you've done every other day of your life.

PEOPLE OF THE WORD ARE ON A MISSION FROM GOD

I often think back to a cartoon that was popular when my husband and I worked in high school ministry. It was called *Pinky and The Brain*. Pinky and the Brain were two lab mice who in every cartoon episode tried by different means to take over the world. Pinky was a dim-witted sidekick, and the Brain was a mean-spirited rodent with a noggin roughly three times the size of a normal mouse. He was something of the anti-Mickey. In each story, the mice would narrowly fail in an attempt at world domination. And at the end of each episode, Pinky would query, "So, what we gonna do tomorrow night, Brain?" To which Brain would always respond, "What we do every night, Pinky, try to take over the world."

Every episode was more laughable than the one before as the mice would implement the Brain's carefully planned strategies. Yet, one had to respect these two in an odd sort of way. They had a mission: "Try to take over the world," and they never veered from it. What would happen if we as individual members of God's church knew our mission so clearly and embraced it so passionately?

People of the Word know that there is one true mission in life, which is the mission Jesus gave.

It is this: Go and make disciples.

It is simple. It is difficult. It is visionary. It gives life purpose.

People of the Word know the mission because they know the Book and they know the Author. Not only that, people of the Word can fulfill the mission because of the Holy Spirit within them. As we have said over and over again, being a person of the Word is more than just knowing the Word intellectually. It is being, in the words of Paul in Romans 12:1–2, transformed by the renewing of our minds.

Have you ever noticed how mixed up we can get on mission in the church? How often do we start thinking of the mission of the church as being material things such as buildings and facilities or even good things such as better programming? Sometimes in our attempt to follow God we confuse changed lives with growing numbers while other times we simply become comfortable staying within our own church walls while the world is literally dying around us.

But what did Jesus say? Yes, I've already tipped my hand on this one, but just to cement this in our hearts, we need to look at His words so we know for sure why we need to be in the Word, to be transformed, and to be set ablaze for His purpose!

Jesus' Mission and Ours

We're going to zip through quite a few passages here because it is imperative that we don't miss what Jesus' mission was and so that we see how our mission ties in with His. We'll look at a number of excerpts from the Gospels and the book of Acts.

LUKE 19:1-10

> He entered Jericho and was passing through. And there was a man called by the name of Zaccheus; he was a chief tax collector and he was rich. Zaccheus was trying to see who Jesus was, and was unable because of the crowd, for he was small in stature. So he ran on ahead and climbed up into a sycamore tree in order to see Him, for He was about to pass through that way. When Jesus came to the place, He looked up and said to him, "Zaccheus, hurry and come down, for today I must stay at your house." And he hurried and came down and received Him gladly. When they saw it, they all [began] to grumble, saying, "He has gone to be the guest of a man who is a sinner." Zaccheus stopped and said to the Lord, "Behold, Lord, half of my possessions I will give to the poor, and if I have defrauded anyone of anything, I will give back four times as much." And Jesus said to him, "Today salvation has come to this house, because he, too, is a son of Abraham. For the Son of Man has come to seek and to save that which was lost."

Questions

1. According to this passage, why did Jesus say that He had come?
2. How did the "religious" people feel about Jesus mode of operation?

While we like to roll our eyes at the behavior of the Pharisees and the religious people of the day, "Pharisaism" is so often the disease that besets those in the church who know the Word intellectually but have somehow held Jesus at arm's length away from their hearts. Those boys knew the Word with their heads, but as is oft repeated, their hearts were far from God. Talk about a scary place to be. Tragically, I believe it is more common in the church than we care to admit. If Jesus was about seeking and saving the lost, our hearts should match the heart of our Savior.

Now, just in case you think that Jesus' comments about seeking and saving the lost were case-specific to Zaccheus, let's check out what Jesus had to say to His disciples just before He ascended back into heaven. Here it is from the first chapter of the book of Acts:

ACTS 1:1-9

> *The first account I composed, Theophilus, about all that Jesus began to do and teach, until the day when he was taken up [to heaven], after He had by the Holy Spirit given orders to the apostles whom He had chosen. To these He also presented Himself alive after His suffering, by many convincing proofs, appearing to them over [a period of] forty days and speaking of the things concerning the kingdom of God. Gathering them together, He commanded them not to leave Jerusalem, but to wait for what the Father had promised, "Which," [He said,] "you heard of from Me; for John baptized with water, but you will be baptized with the Holy Spirit not many days from now."*
>
> *So when they had come together, they were asking Him, saying, "Lord, is it at this time You are restoring the kingdom to Israel?" He said to them, "It is not for you to know times or epochs which the Father has fixed by His own authority; but you will receive power when the Holy Spirit has come upon you; and you shall be My witnesses both in Jerusalem, and in all Judea and Samaria, and even to the remotest part of the earth." And after He had said these things, He was lifted up while they were looking on, and a cloud received Him out of their sight.*

Think about it, when Jesus ascended back to heaven, He didn't say, "Okay boys, the work is done. Why don't you just sit back and chill! Relax and listen to some nice Christian music until I get back." He didn't tell us to just sit back and occupy the four walls we're in. He told us to take the world. The mission was to start in Jerusalem, and to move to Judea, Samaria, and the uttermost parts of the earth.

The next couple of passages we're going to look at from the gospel of John take place shortly before Jesus goes to the cross. Again, note the times Jesus mentions His purpose. Also pay attention to what Jesus says is the way He glorifies His Father.

JOHN 12:23–28

And Jesus answered them, saying, "The hour has come for the Son of Man to be glorified. Truly, truly, I say to you, unless a grain of wheat falls into the earth and dies, it remains alone; but if it dies, it bears much fruit. He who loves his life loses it, and he who hates his life in this world will keep it to life eternal. If anyone serves Me, he must follow Me; and where I am, there My servant will be also; if anyone serves Me, the Father will honor him.

"Now My soul has become troubled; and what shall I say, 'Father, save Me from this hour?' But for this purpose I came to this hour. 'Father, glorify Your name.'" Then a voice came out of heaven: "I have both glorified it, and will glorify it again."

Questions

1. What is the purpose Jesus is referring to in this passage?
2. While we're here, what does Jesus have to say about those who serve Him and follow Him?

This next passage should ring a bell with you as we read through it earlier in the book to see what Jesus had to say about asking things of the Father. This time through, we will be focusing on Jesus purpose—the work He came to do. Don't just breeze by it because you've read it recently; these words are very rich and you would do well to let your soul marinate in them.

JOHN 17:1–19

Jesus spoke these things; and lifting up His eyes to heaven, He said, "Father, the hour has come; glorify Your Son, that the Son my glorify You, even as You gave Him authority over all flesh, that to all whom

You have given Him, He may give eternal life. This eternal life, that they may know You, the only true God, and Jesus Christ whom You have sent. I glorified You on the earth, having accomplished the work which You have given Me to do. Now, Father, glorify Me together with Yourself, with the glory which I had with You before the world was.

"I have manifested Your name to the men whom You gave Me out of the world; they were Yours and You gave them to Me, and they have kept Your word. Now they have come to know that everything You have given Me is from You; for the words which You gave Me I have given to them; and they received [them] and truly understood that I came forth from You, and they believed that You sent Me. I ask on their behalf; I do not ask on behalf of the world, but of those whom You have given Me; for they are Yours; and all things that are Mine are Yours, and Yours are Mine; and I have been glorified in them. I am no longer in the world; and [yet] they themselves are in the world, and I come to You. Holy Father, keep them in Your name, [the name] which You have given Me, that they may be one even as We [are]. While I was with them, I was keeping them in Your name which You have given Me; and I guarded them and not one of them perished but the son of perdition, so that the Scripture would be fulfilled. But now I come to You; and these things I speak in the world so that they may have My joy made full in themselves. I have given them Your word; and the world has hated them, because they are not of the world, even as I am not of the world. I do not ask You to take them out of the world, but to keep them from the evil [one]. They are not of the world, even as I am not of the world. Sanctify them in the truth; Your word is truth. As You sent Me into the world, I also have sent them into the world. For their sakes I sanctify Myself, that they themselves also may be sanctified in truth.

Questions

1. How did Jesus say that He glorified the Father while He was on earth?
2. Mark every occurrence of the word "word(s)" or "truth" and summarize what you learned.
3. What does Jesus have to say about being sent and sending?
4. What applications can you draw?

This final section of John 17 always blows me away because in it I see that Jesus is praying specifically for me, as I am one of those who have believed through the words of the disciples passed down in the Bible.

JOHN 17:20-26

I do not ask on behalf of these alone, but for those also who believe in Me through their word; that they may all be one; even as You, Father, [are] in Me and I in You, that they also may be in Us, so that the world may believe that You sent Me. The glory which You have given Me I have given to them, that they may be one, just as We are one; I in them and You in Me, that they may be perfected in unity, so that the world may know that You sent Me, and loved them, even as You have loved Me. Father, I desire that they also, whom You have given Me, be with Me where I am, so that they may see My glory which You have given Me, for You loved Me before the foundation of the world.

O righteous Father, although the world has not known You, yet I have known You; and these have known that You sent Me; and I have made Your name known to them, and will make it known, so that the love with which You loved Me may be in them, and I in them.

Questions

1. Is Jesus praying for you in this passage? Have you believed?
2. If you have believed, what is His prayer for you? What should mark your life?

Love and Unity. If you know the facts about the Bible, you can teach people the facts about the Bible. If you are a disciple of the Master, not only knowing His words but also having His words abiding in you and transforming you will cause you to reproduce after your own kind. You will become as Jesus put it "a fisher of men." Jesus actually prays to the Father before His crucifixion that His people will be marked by two distinct characteristics: love and unity. We don't always like that because in a fallen world it takes the empowering of the Holy Spirit to walk in a life of love and unity. It would seem at times as though this is truly an impossible mission.

Mission Impossible. Have you ever wondered why the mission on which we have been sent seems like mission impossible? Why walking in the way of Jesus is such hard work? Why evangelism and discipleship are so tough? It is because they are impossible tasks apart from the transformational work of the Holy Spirit and the power of the Holy Spirit unleashed in our lives. You can't do it just on will power. It doesn't matter how much grit and tenacity you have. You can't do it with simple head knowledge of the Bible. It doesn't matter if your Bible IQ dwarfs that of those around you. You do it by walking in the Spirit, by walking with God day by day in His power. But how many of us who claim the name "Christian" live with the power of the Holy Spirit truly unleashed in our lives?

How many of us routinely and regularly are yielding the fruit of the Spirit: love, joy, peace, patience, kindness, goodness, faithfulness, gentleness, and self-control?

I know that in my life I have, over the years, been an expert at quenching the Spirit and walking in my own "power" apart from the Word of God, sometimes willfully, but usually in something of an accidental, unintentional daze because I had not been intentionally in the Word of God and prayer.

It is this dynamic relationship with God that sets our souls ablaze! It is living in His presence through His Word and prayer that fills us with holy passion and empowers us for the mission that He has given us to fulfill.

Think about the life of Jesus for a minute and consider how He depended on God the Father throughout His life on earth. Remember that although He was fully human, He was still fully God, and yet watch how He fully depends on the Father and on the Word. It is amazing, and it is convicting to me that I have the audacity to think I can function with any less.

Knowing the Word of God is only effective if it leads us to knowing the God of the Word. You can have an intellectual grasp on the Word of God without being a person of the Word. I know, it's sad, but it's true. Just studying is not a guarantee that the Word will take root. That can be empirically proven by looking at the lives of many people. We can handle it with gloved hands and keep it essentially at arm's length. It happens. It breaks my heart, but it happens.

When God does His transformational work in our lives, though, He never leaves Bible knowledge locked up in our heads. Don't miss the point, knowing the Word is critical because the Bible is the key place we hear God. It is His revealed Word. It is through this Word that God cleans and transforms and changes us into zealous lovers of God, spiritually impassioned people who love the Lord our God with all of our heart, soul, strength, and mind, and our neighbors as ourselves. This is the way of the Word...loving God and loving others!

It is in the Word that we learn to love like Jesus. It is in the Word that we learn how short we fall but also how miraculously He has shown mercy and love. It is through the Word that God molds us in such a way that we become little by little more like Jesus, little by little more spiritually impassioned and contagious, ready to influence this world and accomplish our mission from God!

Drawing Near

This week's activities are designed to help you continue to draw near to God on a regular basis long after you close the pages of this book.

* Find a friend or mentor who will keep you accountable in your Bible reading. Resolve to make the contact this week.
* Sign up for the Deep & Wide e-group at www.deepandwide.org that will give you weekly tips and encouragement in your Bible reading.
* Start a read-through-the-Bible small group. You could plan to meet monthly to benchmark progress.
* If reading isn't your thing, purchase the Bible on CD and begin to work it into your routine. Again, do it this next week.
* Take an hour or two at your favorite coffee shop, restaurant, or park to do some "chunk" reading in the Word. Give God a couple hours of your time, and you'll be amazed at what He can do with it!

Bible Study Tool Box

Five-Minute Survey of the Old Testament

In the beginning God creates. Adam is the first man created, Eve the first woman. They are created by God without sin but are quickly deceived in the Garden of Eden by the serpent (later identified as Satan). Eve actually eats the forbidden fruit (from the tree of the knowledge of good and evil) first and gives it to her husband Adam. Through this act of sin, death enters the world. Adam and Eve are banished from the beautiful garden, so they cannot eat of the tree of life which would cause them to live eternally in a state of alienation from God.

Although man rebels against God, God immediately predicts the coming of a Savior who will crush the head of the serpent (Messianic Covenant). This prophecy is later fulfilled in the person of Jesus Christ. However, in the meantime, sin has entered into the world, and death through sin.

Adam and Eve have many children, the most famous of them are the first two, Cain and Abel. Cain, resentful that God had accepted Abel's sacrifice and not his own, kills Abel, and sin really starts rolling. Things continue to go downhill from here until God has simply had enough.

Saying that He regrets having made man, God calls Noah to build an ark so that He can save him and his family from the coming destruction of the world by means of a flood. Noah obeys and God saves him, his wife, his three sons, and their wives. After the Flood, God puts a rainbow in the sky as a sign of His covenant with all living creatures that He will never again destroy the entire earth with a flood.

Noah's sons, Japheth, Shem, and Ham become the fathers of all the nations. Over time, the population of the world increases, and the people again begin to go off course when in their pride they determine to build a tower that will reach to heaven. In the midst of the construction, God confuses their languages, thereby thwarting their plans.

The next major player on the scene is Abraham, originally known as Abram. Abram and his wife Sarai (whose name is later changed to Sarah) live in the land of Ur. God tells Abram that he must leave the land that he is living in to go to a land that God will show him. Abram trusts God and goes, taking with him his wife and household. Although God changes his name to Abraham and promises to make him a great nation, Abraham finds himself really old with no children.

Taking matters into her own hands, Sarah decides to play God. She gives her handmaiden Hagar to Abraham so that the promise might be fulfilled through her seed on behalf of Sarah. Not a good idea. Hagar bears Abraham a son named Ishmael and Sarah is steamed.

Eventually, God does bless Sarah with a son in her old age. His name is Isaac, and it is through him that God chooses to fulfill His promise to Abraham. Like his father before him, Isaac finds himself in possession of a promise to be a great nation but without a child for quite some time. Isaac, though, prays for his wife Rebekah, and God causes her to conceive twins, Esau and Jacob.

These babies certainly weren't twins of the identical variety. Esau was a tough, manly man, though an aisle shy in the brains department, while Jacob was an instigating, conniving, mama's boy. Although older, Esau lost both his birthright and blessing due to the trickery of his younger brother. Let's just say it's a good thing that they didn't have to look across the table at each other at Christmas dinner.

Warts and all, Jacob is God's chosen brother. Any guesses as to what Jacob's name becomes? That's right, Israel! Hence, the nation of Israel.

(See, this isn't so hard, is it?) Rather appropriately, Jacob ends up with an extra wife after his uncle (also his new father-in-law) pulls a wedding day bait-and-switch on him. Thus, from Jacob, his wives Leah and Rachel, and their handmaidens are born what we know as the twelve tribes of Israel.

The most famous of Jacob's children is his son Joseph, the guy with the amazing technicolor dreamcoat. His father's favorite, Joseph was sold by his brothers into slavery in Egypt. Eventually, God raises Joseph up to second in command in all of Egypt. He is reunited with his family who then comes to live with him in Egypt.

After Joseph dies, everything is still fine until eventually a Pharaoh rises to power who does not remember Joseph and the way God used him to save Egypt. This Pharaoh decides to enslave the family of Joseph, now called the Hebrews, who have grown to great numbers in the land. The Hebrews remain in bondage for 400 years until the time of Moses.

Because the Hebrew population in Egypt has grown so rapidly, the Egyptian Pharaoh issues a decree that all male Hebrew babies should be killed. He fears that the slaves may turn against him should a foreign country invade. During this time, the mother of Moses hides her newborn son in a basket and sets it in the river to save him. The Pharaoh's daughter sees the basket with the infant and adopts him, raising him as her own. As an adult, young Moses intervenes in a fight between an Egyptian and one of his Hebrew brothers, killing the Egyptian. He subsequently flees Egypt and becomes a shepherd for forty years until God calls to him from a burning bush to go back and deliver the Hebrews from Egypt.

Although resistant at first, Moses eventually obeys and after a series of ten plagues and the Passover, he leads the Hebrews out of Egypt and on their way to the Promised Land. On the way, God parts the Red Sea; He feeds them with manna, and leads them with a cloud by day and a pillar of fire at night. Although they get to the Promised Land quickly, ten of the twelve spies sent into the land report that giants occupy the land. They shrink back in fear instead of trusting God's promise. Thus, God makes them wander in the wilderness for forty years before they are finally allowed to enter the Promised Land.

Moses sees the Promised Land from afar, but it is Joshua who leads the people into the Promised Land. Under his leadership, the famed walls of Jericho fall and the people, more or less, follow God. When Joshua dies, however, the people return to their wandering ways, having not driven out all of the people from the lands that they had conquered.

Into this rebellious situation, God sends the judges to help save the people when they call out to Him for help. Some of the more notable judges include Deborah, Gideon, Samson, and Samuel.

During the time of Samuel, however, the people of Israel cry out for a king so they will be like the other nations around them. Bad move. For in asking for a king, God says they are in effect rejecting not Samuel as a judge, but God, Himself, as their king. Israel which has been up to this point a theocracy, a government with God as king, now changes to a monarchy as God gives the people a king in the man Saul.

While Saul starts out as a hesitant king, even hiding from the masses at the beginning, he becomes quite full of himself before long and falls out of favor with God by his blatant disobedience. Because of his rebellion, God chooses another to be king in Saul's place. The man God chooses is not a descendant of Saul, but a shepherd named David.

Before David becomes king, we hear of his exploits in killing the giant Goliath and of his deep friendship with Jonathan, King Saul's son, and of his first marriage to King Saul's daughter, Michal. Pursued ferociously by King Saul because he is perceived as such a threat to his kingdom, David lives on the edge for several years before King Saul finally takes his own life in battle, and David ascends to the throne.

Called a "man after God's own heart," David's life exemplifies what it means to seek and follow God, with the exception of the Bathsheba incident. Bathsheba was married to one of David's soldiers, Uriah. One day, when David's men are out fighting wars, David is home in his palace. From his high vantage point, he sees Bathsheba bathing. Immediately taken by her beauty, David sends for her. One thing quickly leads to another and before long, David is sitting in a soap opera of adultery and murder, having offed Uriah upon receiving the news of Bathsheba's pregnancy.

The prophet Nathan calls David on his sin, and David repents immediately. The damage having been done, David takes Bathsheba as another wife. After losing the baby conceived in adultery, Bathsheba eventually bears David his son, Solomon. Solomon succeeds his father David as king, but not before some of David's other sons, most notably Absalom, make a run at the throne.

It is Solomon who finally builds a permanent temple for the Lord. David had not been allowed to do this because, although he had followed God with all of his heart, he had been a man of bloodshed, a man of war. Solomon is best remembered for his wealth and his wisdom in ruling, but ironically, it is his lack of wisdom in the area of women that becomes his undoing.

Having wives and concubines that numbered in the hundreds, Solomon accommodated his foreign wives in the area of idol worship. Bad idea. Solomon is succeeded by his son, Rehoboam, who is not a good man. In fact, he is so bad that God tears a large portion of the kingdom out of his hand, leaving him only a small part because of His promise to David.

This is where it gets a little complicated, but once you grasp this, so much of the Old Testament will begin to hold together for you. Under Saul, David, and Solomon, Israel was one country with one king, the united monarchy with all twelve tribes of Israel under the king's control. When God pulls part of the kingdom away from Rehoboam, we move into the time of the divided monarchy. Rehoboam is still the king of what becomes known as the Southern Kingdom or Judah (comprised of the two tribes of Judah and Benjamin), while the Northern Kingdom or Israel (comprised of the other ten tribes) is given to a man named

Jeroboam. The capital of the Southern Kingdom is Jerusalem; the capital of the Northern Kingdom is Samaria. Details? Yes. Important? Extremely.

Until you grasp this flow of history around the division of the kingdom, much of the Old Testament history and prophecy will stay extremely muddy. With a reasonable understanding of this, however, you can jump in and read anywhere in the Old Testament with at least some degree of ease. So, because of the importance of this, let's quickly review:

Northern Kingdom	Southern Kingdom
✦ Israel	✦ Judah
✦ 10 Tribes	✦ 2 Tribes
✦ Non-Davidic	✦ Davidic Line
✦ Capital: Samaria	✦ Capital: Jerusalem

Once the kingdom divides a series of kings follow. The kings of Israel are bad. They are always bad. Not one of them is even remotely good. Israel, all bad, all the time.

The kings of Judah, on the other hand, are a mixed bag. Some are horrible, others okay, and at least one you could name a child after. More are bad than good, and most of the good ones still have reasonable shortcomings, but as a group, they prove to be better than Israel, which is why the ax falls on them later than it does on their brothers to the North.

Elijah and Elisha prophesy during the time of the divided kingdom. The other prophets are sprinkled throughout the times of the monarchy, the captivity, and the post-exile period.

If you hate historical dates, you may be inclined to skip over the next section, but I implore you, please don't. Unlike most history that is fraught with countless crucial dates, there are only two dates that you need to remember in studying the Old Testament. The first is 722 BC, the second, 586 BC.

In 722 BC, the nation of Assyria conquered and deported the Northern Kingdom of Israel as was prophesied. After deporting Israel and dispersing the people, Assyria resettled other people groups in the land of Israel. These people then intermarried with the remaining Israelites creating a half-breed people group referred to as Samaritans. This becomes significant in the New Testament as we see the intense hatred that the "pure-bred" Jews had for their half-breed brothers. Due to the deportation and intermixing of the Northern Kingdom, these tribes are often referred to as the ten lost tribes of Israel.

Seeing their brothers carried away by Assyria does not have the impact on the Southern Kingdom that it should have. Although it takes a little longer and though there are pockets of revival along the way, notably that of King Josiah, eventually Judah goes the way of Israel. In 586 BC, Nebuchadnezzar conquers Judah and takes the people away into captivity in Babylon.

One of the people carried off to Babylon is Daniel. Probably the best known vegetable-eater of all time, Daniel, along with his three friends Shadrach, Meshach, and Abednego, were made servants in Babylon. Shadrach, Meshach, and Abednego were thrown into a fiery furnace when they refused to bow down to a golden statue only to be saved by the power of God. Daniel, likewise, was thrown into a den of lions because he continued to pray to his God even when prayer to anyone but the king had been outlawed. He, too, was saved by the power of God.

After seventy years of captivity in Babylon, the people of Judah are released to go back to Jerusalem.

Nehemiah is in charge of rebuilding the wrecked walls of the city.

Between the end of the Old Testament and the beginning of the New Testament is a period of 400 years often referred to as the silent years.

With the Christ-event, God again speaks to His people beginning with His Word to Zechariah foretelling of the coming of John the Baptist who would prepare the way of the Lord.

Quick Book Summaries

Whatever you do, don't read these quickie summaries and think you've got yourself a handle on the whole Bible! Remember, I'm not a PhD, ThD or any other "D"! I'm still a learner myself. So, from one learner to another, here are some observations on what you'll find in the books of the Bible, and if the books are "easy" to read, "moderate" in difficulty, or just plain "difficult" on the subjective Pam-scale. Remember, "difficult" doesn't mean you can't understand them, just that they might not be crystal clear the first (or second) time around, and "easy" doesn't mean that there won't be any sticky issues of interpretation or application!

OLD TESTAMENT

THE BOOKS OF THE LAW

Genesis – Starts with the creation of the earth. Major storyline follows the lives of Adam, Noah, Abraham, Isaac, Jacob, and Joseph. Fifty chapters. Easy reading.

Exodus – Begins in Egypt with a new king (pharaoh) coming to power who did not know Joseph and what he had done for Egypt. Tells of the enslavement of the Israelites and their eventual exodus (leaving) from Egypt by the power of God. The main human character in the book is Moses. In Exodus, we have the giving of the Law at Mt. Sinai and the institution of the tabernacle with a great deal of instructions relating to it, its contents, and the priests. The low point of the book is the making of the golden calf while Moses is receiving the Law from God. Forty chapters. Moderate reading.

Leviticus – Rules and regulations for Israel! What sacrifices were required? What was required of the priest? Of the people? In the book of Leviticus we see what was required of a sinful people in the presence of a holy God. This book is often the undoing of people who try to read through the Bible in a linear fashion. Twenty-seven chapters. Difficult reading.

Numbers – Yes, Numbers has lots of numbers as the people are "numbered" by tribe and more instructions are given on sacrifices and offerings. But for a book that starts off with less than a bang, Numbers boasts some extremely memorable accounts from the wilderness wanderings, including Miriam (the sister of Moses) being struck with leprosy, Israel sending the spies into the promised land, and Korah, a rebellious Levite, being swallowed alive by the ground (bet you never heard that story in Sunday School!). Numbers also includes such memorable stories as the bronze serpent in the wilderness and the talking donkey of Balaam. Thirty-six chapters. Moderate reading.

Deuteronomy – Moses' life is drawing to a close and the children of Israel are just about to enter the Promised Land under the leadership of Joshua. With this background, Moses speaks to Israel reminding them of the works of God and calling them to obedience to the covenant and laying out for them the blessings and curses associated with keeping or breaking the covenant. After giving the commands to Israel on the east side of the Jordan River, Moses dies at the end of the book, being remembered in Deuteronomy 34:10b as one whom "the Lord knew face to face." Thirty-four chapters. Moderate reading.

HISTORY

Joshua – What an AWESOME book! God leads Joshua (the successor to Moses) and the people of Israel across the parted Jordan River and into the land which He had promised to Abraham way back in Genesis. In this historical book, we find the familiar stories of Rahab the harlot and the toppling of the walls of Jericho. We also meet the incredible spy, Caleb, who followed the Lord fully! Throughout the book, we see both the results of obedience and the results of sinful actions. Twenty-four chapters. Easy reading (with the exception of a few chapters on the division of the land among the tribes of Israel).

Judges – After the death of Joshua, individual judges raised up by God lead the people of Israel. Judges is a book of cycles. The people forget God and sin against Him. God brings judgment against them in the form of oppression from another nation. When the people wake up and cry out to God for help, God sends a deliverer for them. They typically behave well enough while the judge is alive and then upon the death of the judge fall away and get thumped again. Some of the more memorable judges include: Deborah, Gideon, and Samson. Twenty-one chapters. Easy reading.

Ruth – Biography of Ruth, a Moabite woman who becomes part of the line of Christ. Her faithfulness to her Israelite mother-in-law Naomi is legendary. Ruth marries the son of Naomi when Naomi, her husband, and two sons come to live in the land of Moab during a famine in Israel. While in Moab, Naomi's husband dies. Later, when both of her sons die, she decides to return to Israel. Ruth insists on going with her and the rest is history. Four chapters. Easy reading.

I Samuel – The book begins with the life of Samuel, the last judge in Israel, and ends with the life and death of Saul, the first king in Israel. Although mentioned in the lineage in the book of Ruth, David makes his first appearance in I Samuel. He kills Goliath, strikes up a friendship with Jonathan (King Saul's son), and spends much of the book fleeing from King Saul. Thirty-one chapters. Easy reading.

II Samuel – II Samuel follows the ascension to power and life of King David. It includes the story of David and Bathsheba, and the death of David's son Absalom. Ending on an uncharacteristic low note in David's life (right down there, so to speak, with the Bathsheba event), the book draws to a close with the wrath of God being poured out against Israel in the form of pestilence in the land for three days as a result of David's sin of taking a census and numbering the people. Twenty-four chapters. Easy reading.

I Kings – Beginning with the death of King David, I Kings follows the kingdom of Israel under David's son, King Solomon as he asks wisdom of God and subsequently builds the temple at Jerusalem. In spite of all his wisdom, Solomon allows foreign women and their gods to turn his heart from the Lord. Because of this, God divides the kingdom under Solomon's arrogant son, Rehoboam, leaving David's line to rule the Southern Kingdom of two tribes (Judah and Benjamin) often called Judah. The Northern Kingdom of the other ten tribes retains the name Israel. The remainder of the book tells of the exploits of the kings of Judah and Israel, as well as accounts of the prophets Elijah and Elisha. The book ends with the account of King Ahaziah in Israel and the content continues right into the beginning of II Kings. Twenty-two chapters. Easy reading.

II Kings – A continuation of I Kings, this book follows the kings and kingdom of Israel up to their defeat and deportation by Assyria in 722 BC, and follows Judah to the time of the Babylonian captivity in 586 BC. The taking up of Elijah and the ministry of Elisha are also covered in II Kings. Twenty-five chapters. Easy reading.

I Chronicles – Heavy on the genealogies for the first nine chapters, then moves into chronicling the life of King David for much of the book. Twenty-nine chapters. Difficult reading in chapters 1–9 and 23–27. Easy reading remainder of book.

II Chronicles – Beginning with Solomon and the building of the Temple, II Chronicles tells of the subsequent kings of Israel and Judah, following Judah all the way to the time of Cyrus king of Persia who conquered the Babylonian Empire. Judah had been taken into captivity in Babylon in 586 BC. Thirty-six chapters. Moderate reading.

Ezra – Ezra continues the historical account, picking up the story of the people of Judah who are in captivity in Babylon and how a group is sent back to Jerusalem by King Cyrus of Persia to rebuild the temple. Ten chapters. Moderate reading.

Nehemiah – The book of Nehemiah tells of the reconstructing of the wall of Jerusalem and the renewing of the covenant after the Babylonian exile. Thirteen chapters. Moderate reading.

Esther – This book tells the story of Queen Esther, a Jewess who unwittingly became Queen of Persia and saved her people from extermination at the hands of the wicked Haman. Ten chapters. Easy reading.

POETRY AND WISDOM LITERATURE

Job – Why do bad things happen to good people? Even people who don't read the Bible know what it means to suffer like Job. This godly man loses everything, but remains faithful to God through severe trials and tragedies. In the end, God restores his health and possessions, but it is a long time in coming. Forty-two chapters. Difficult reading.

Psalms – What a book of worship! King David wrote many of the psalms and as you read, you'll recognize that many of our current worship songs are lifted directly from this portion of the Bible. One hundred fifty chapters. Easy reading.

Proverbs – While many of the psalms are attributed to David, his son, Solomon wrote much of Proverbs. The Proverbs give practical advice on living, not promises per se but the results that generally follow from a given set of actions. Thirty-one chapters. Easy reading.

Ecclesiastes – Written by Solomon, a man who had everything, Ecclesiastes concludes that all life has to offer apart from God is vanity. Twelve chapters. Moderate reading.

Song of Solomon – A love story written by Solomon. Shows the high biblical view of physical love within marriage. Not a good place to start your children reading the Bible. Eight chapters. Moderate reading.

MAJOR PROPHETS

Isaiah – Writing to the Southern Kingdom of Judah before they are taken into captivity by Babylon, Isaiah not only warns of coming judgment, but also has much to say about the coming Messiah and the millennial kingdom. Tradition says that Isaiah was eventually martyred by being sawn in two. Sixty-six chapters. Difficult reading.

Jeremiah – Jeremiah also prophesied to Judah, but after the time of Isaiah. Jeremiah is often referred to as the weeping prophet. He continually characterizes Judah having stiff necks and ears that will not listen. They are stubborn with evil hearts, yet we have in this prophet the view toward the new covenant when God will write His laws on the hearts of His people (Jeremiah 31) and cause them to walk in His ways. Fifty-two chapters. Difficult reading.

Lamentations – Generally attributed to Jeremiah, the book of Lamentations laments the fall of Jerusalem to Babylon. Five chapters. Moderate reading.

Ezekiel – Ezekiel prophesied to the people of Judah who had been taken into captivity in Babylon. This book features great visions of God, but the end of the book is very difficult to wade through as it is a very detailed description of a yet future temple, probably during the millennial kingdom. Forty-eight chapters. Difficult reading.

Daniel – Taken into captivity in Babylon during his youth, Daniel rose to power under different leaders, but never compromised in his unswerving devotion to his God. The book of Daniel contains some difficult prophetic sections, in addition to the well-known stories of Daniel in the lion's den and Shadrach, Meshach, and Abednego in the fiery furnace. Twelve chapters. Mixture of easy and difficult reading.

MINOR PROPHETS

Hosea – Don't like your job? Just consider the job this guy is given. God tells Hosea to marry a prostitute as a picture of God's faithful love to Israel even though she is continually unfaithful to Him. Hosea prophesied to the Northern Kingdom of Israel. Fourteen chapters. Moderate reading.

Joel – Joel writes to Judah, the Southern Kingdom, prior to the Babylonian captivity and speaks of locusts, destruction, and ultimate deliverance. Three chapters. Moderate reading.

Amos – A shepherd from Judah, Amos was sent to prophesy to the Northern Kingdom of Israel prior to their fall to Assyria. Nine chapters. Moderate reading.

Obadiah – Obadiah prophesies against the descendants of Esau, the people of Edom. One chapter. Moderate reading.

Jonah – Jonah, probably the most famous of the minor prophets, is sent not to the people of Israel or Judah, but to the wicked city of Ninevah. When he decides not to do his job, Jonah is swallowed by a great fish before he finally repents and delivers the message God has for him to give. Four chapters. Easy reading.

Micah Micah of Moresheth prophesied to Judah well before the Babylonian captivity. He speaks of coming judgment, but also of a coming ruler "From the days of eternity," who will go forth from Bethlehem. Hmm, wonder who that could be? Seven chapters. Moderate reading.

Nahum – Nahum prophesies to Judah, the Southern Kingdom, prior to the Babylonian captivity. His message is the coming judgment against Ninevah, the capital of Samaria that had conquered the Northern Kingdom of Israel. Three chapters. Moderate reading.

Habakkuk – Habakkuk prophesies to Judah of the impending judgment coming at the hand of Babylon. He questions why God is using evil Babylon to judge His people. Three chapters. Moderate reading.

Zephaniah – Another prophet to Judah, Zephaniah also spoke of the come judgment by Babylon, yet looks forward to the blessings of the millennial kingdom. Three chapters. Moderate reading.

Haggai – Haggai wrote after the Babylonian Exile to call the people to finish the reconstruction of the temple. Two chapters. Moderate reading.

Zechariah – Like Haggai, Zechariah called the people to finish rebuilding the temple. Zechariah is filled with many references to the coming Messiah. Fourteen chapters. Moderate reading.

Malachi – Malachi wrote after the people had returned from captivity to their homeland. Apparently conquest by their enemies was far enough in the past that the people were once again drifting away from God. Four chapters. Moderate reading.

New Testament

THE GOSPELS

Matthew, Mark, and Luke are often termed the synoptic Gospels. They each chronicle the life of Jesus Christ but aim at different audiences. In the synoptics, some accounts are recorded by all three evangelists, some by two, others by only one of the three.

Matthew – Matthew wrote to a Jewish audience. The Sermon on the Mount appears in Matthew 5–7. Much of Jesus' teaching in this gospel has to do with what the kingdom of God is like. It is like a mustard seed, like leaven, like a treasure hidden in a field. Twenty-eight chapters. Easy reading.

Mark – Mark wrote to a Roman audience. He also wrote, by far, the shortest of the gospel accounts. Sixteen chapters. Easy reading.

Luke – Luke, the physician, wrote to "Theophilus," his Greek, Gentile friend. Luke is also the author of the book of Acts. Luke features the Christmas story that may be read at your house on Christmas Eve, it always is at mine, that is found in Luke 2:1–20. Also notable in Luke is the story of Zaccheus, (the wee little man). Twenty-four chapters. Easy reading.

John – John the Apostle takes a different approach in writing his gospel. He tells us that he has written "that you may believe that Jesus is the Christ, the Son of God; and that believing, you may have life in His name" (John 20:31b). Unlike the synoptic Gospels that take a more chronological approach, John's outline follows seven major signs performed by Jesus. Twenty-wonderful chapters. Easy reading.

THE HISTORY OF THE EARLY CHURCH

Acts – In Acts, Luke, the author of the gospel bearing his name, recounts the birth of the church. He tells of the ascension of Christ, the coming of the Holy Spirit, the martyrdom of Stephen, the preaching of Peter, and the conversion and subsequent ministry of Paul. Twenty-eight chapters. Easy reading.

THE EPISTLES (LETTERS)

Romans – In his most thorough discussion of doctrine, Paul explains the righteousness of God in the letter to the Romans. Excellent book to ground new Christians. Sixteen chapters. Moderate reading.

I Corinthians – You think your church has problems? The church at Corinth had issues out the ears! In this letter, Paul discusses such issues as divisions in the church, problems of gross immorality, marriage and divorce, as well as other topics. Sixteen chapters. Easy reading.

II Corinthians – Really, you have to figure a church with as many problems as Corinth was going to take more than one letter! Thirteen chapters. Easy reading.

Galatians – Confused on the relationship of the Christian to the Law? Galatians is the book for you! Often considered a mini-Romans, Paul emphasizes that the way to God is through faith alone, not working your way to Him. This is the book where you'll find the fruit of the Spirit listed. Six chapters. Easy reading.

Ephesians – Paul writes the church at Ephesus telling them who they are "in Christ," and what this means as they live their lives. Six chapters. Easy reading.

Philippians – In the letter to the Philippians, Paul covers topics including joy, unity, and humility. Four chapters. Easy reading.

Colossians – Need to brush up on the person and work of Jesus Christ? Soak in Colossians for a couple of weeks! Four chapters. Easy reading.

I Thessalonians – Unlike the Corinthian church, the church at Thessalonica was apparently "doing the job," and Paul tells them to "excel still more." In addition to other topics, Paul addresses the question of the day of the Lord. Five chapters. Easy reading.

II Thessalonians – Paul spends much of this epistle setting people straight on the day of the Lord. Three chapters. Moderate reading.

I Timothy – Paul packs a number of contemporary issues in this one as he addresses the topics of church leadership and women in the church. Six chapters. Easy reading.

II Timothy – Just before his martyr's death, Paul writes to his son in the faith, Timothy, to pass the baton and remind him to guard the gospel with which he has been entrusted, and to pass it along to faithful men who will be able to teach others also. Four chapters. Easy reading.

Titus – Paul writes to tell Titus to exhort the church in sound doctrine and to engage in good deeds. He is to appoint elders and instruct those in the church on how to live in a manner that honors Christ. Three chapters. Easy reading.

Philemon – This is a personal letter from Paul to Philemon regarding his runaway slave Onesimus, who had come to faith in Christ. One chapter. Easy reading.

Hebrews – The author of Hebrews exhorts what is probably a primarily Jewish church facing persecution to consider Jesus, its merciful and faithful high priest who is able to save forever. Knowing this, they are to hold fast, to draw near, and to press on to maturity. Thirteen chapters. Some difficult subject matter, but wonderful reading.

James – I always get a good "toe-steppin'" from the book of James. Sure, the first thing that many associate with James is the concept of faith and works, but it's always the teaching on the tongue that has me confessing. Five chapters. Easy reading.

I Peter – The apostle Peter speaks of topics including the relationship of the husband and wife, and the issue of suffering in the lives of those who follow Christ. Five chapters. Easy reading.

II Peter – In a letter that has many similarities to Jude's, Peter stresses the concept of true knowledge of God in the face of false teachers. Three chapters. Easy reading.

I John – Wondering if you really have eternal life? Read I John; that's why the apostle John wrote this letter. Five chapters. Easy reading (even in Greek).

II John – In this short letter, John talks about walking in the truth and abiding in the teaching of Christ. One chapter. Easy reading.

III John – This is a personal letter from the apostle John to a man named Gaius dealing with a specific problem in the church. One chapter. Easy reading.

Jude – Jude, the half-brother of Jesus, writes to tell the church to contend earnestly for the faith. He warns of coming judgment citing numerous Old Testament examples yet assures that God is able to keep them from stumbling and to make them stand before His presence blameless with great joy. One chapter. Moderate reading.

PROPHECY

Revelation – The apostle John writes a prophetic book that has yet to see its ultimate fulfillment. Awesome pictures of heaven and exhortations to endure. Do I understand it all? No. Do I love it? Yes. By the way, I hear the Precept courses on Revelation are excellent! Twenty-two chapters. Difficult reading, but worthwhile if for no other reason (and there are many other reasons) than to see the descriptions of the throne of God and of heaven. Let me whet your appetite:

> *And I saw no temple in it, for the Lord God the Almighty and the Lamb are its temple. And the city has no need of the sun or of the moon to shine on it, for the glory of God has illumined it, and its lamp [is] the Lamb. (Revelation 21:22–23)*

Ablaze

What Being Set Ablaze Looks Like

Inductive Studies on Biblical Examples
of Spiritual Passion

In this section, we are going to dig a little deeper and look at a few examples from the Bible to see what lessons we can glean from people whom God set ablaze for His purposes.

Okay, about now, if you're at all like me, you're thinking about throwing a full-fledged pity party, complete with invitations, decorations, and matching napkins. Right? Sure Bible guys could shine because, well, look at them; they were just this side of perfect. Moses, for one, actually hung out in the presence of God, and even though Peter and John were uneducated fishermen, they got to pal around with Jesus all those years, and Daniel was, well, Daniel. Spiritual passion for them must have been as hard as falling off a slick log. Of course these guys had passion and influence, but how does that translate to me? Good question. I'm so glad you asked!

Actually, the more I read the Word of God, the more hope I have because nearly all of the heroes of the faith have some not-so-great moments on the record. Daniel, you ask? Okay, even God said that Daniel was all that and a bag of chips (my translation). Obviously, he was not perfect because the Bible tells us categorically that all have sinned and fallen short of the glory of God. Nevertheless, God shows us in His Word time and again that abiding in the presence of God brings true and noticeable change to the lives of His followers.

DANIEL

Daniel was one of those followers. He was a man who the Babylonians knew as having in him "the spirit of the holy gods." He was also known as a man who constantly served God. In Daniel, we see a man who rose to the top levels of every government that came to town, yet the king addressed him twice in regard to his constant service of God.

Before we go to the Bible, let's set some basic historical context. In 586 BC, Babylon conquered Judah, the southern part of Israel, and took many of the people into a seventy-year captivity. Daniel was one of the captives. He was trained for three years to serve the king of Babylon and had every opportunity to become absorbed into the Babylonian "good life." Daniel, though, stood for God day in and day out while continuing to serve the king with integrity and prowess.

So what made Daniel, well, Daniel? That is what we are going to try and discover as we look to the Word of God. In this first character study, we'll focus on Daniel chapters six and nine. Chapter six recounts Daniel's continued prayer life in the face of a law forbidding it. You may recognize it as the account of Daniel in the lion's den.

As you read Daniel 6, ask questions of the text as you go along. For example: Who are the main characters? What is going on? Where is the situation unfolding? Why is the incident occurring? And what does that tell us about the main characters? When is this happening? How do the characters behave/react?

Also, as you read, mark any references to Daniel by circling or underlining his name and any pronouns (he, his, etc.) referring to him.

Read Daniel 6:1–28 and consider the following:

1. Looking back at the text, list everything that you learned about Daniel in this chapter.

2. What kind of an employee or government official do you think he'd make? Why?

3. What, then, motivated his political opponents?

4. What, specifically, did others say about Daniel? Note what was said and who said it.

5. What was the king's reaction? Did he perceive the actions of Daniel as insubordination? Why/why not?

6. How does Daniel react in the face of the injustice?

7. What is the "take home" lesson for King Darius?

8. In what specific ways could your life look more like Daniel's?

Next let's look at Daniel 9:1–23. Though not as famous, this text provides an intimate look into the prayer life a man of unparalleled passion and devotion. As you read, remember to ask yourself the Who, What, Where, Why, When, and How questions. Also, pay special attention to why Daniel is praying and what he is basing his prayers upon.

Read Daniel 9:1–23 and consider the following:

1. What do you learn about Daniel from this chapter?

2. Describe the setting in which Daniel and his fellow countrymen find themselves.

3. According to the text of chapter nine, what reason does Daniel give for their situation?

4. What does Daniel understand from the Law of Moses?

5. What is Daniel praying for in this chapter? Where does he get the idea to pray in this way?

If you answered that Daniel got the idea to pray from the prophet Jeremiah, you'd be right! Daniel prayed the Word of God! Let's take a minute and look at what God's words to Jeremiah were regarding the

seventy years of captivity. Yes, we're looking at a bunch of scripture...
isn't it great?

Read Jeremiah 29:1–14 and consider the following:
1. What were God's instructions through the prophet Jeremiah to His
   people regarding the Babylonian captivity?
2. How long was the captivity supposed to last?
3. How do these instructions compare with the prayer that Daniel offered to God?
4. What application can you make to your own prayer life based on
   what you have studied here?

PETER AND JOHN

Quite unlike Daniel who was highly trained and educated, Peter and
John were simple fishermen. There was nothing in and of themselves
that should have made these two stick out in a crowd, except the fact that
they knew the One in whose presence they had walked and whose Spirit
now indwelled them. These were men who, fearing for their own lives,
had scattered at the arrest of Jesus but who, thereafter, were empowered
and spoke with boldness and confidence. Let's look a little closer at these
flawed and yet supernaturally transformed men.

Read Acts 4:1–13 and consider the following:
1. Mark every occurrence of "Peter" and "John" and any pronouns associated with them. Then, list what you learn about Peter and John
   from this passage.
2. How would you describe these men? What characterized them?
3. What did the people recognize about Peter and John?
4. Could what was said about Peter and John also be said of you? Why
   or why not?

Read Acts 2:1–47 and consider the following:

1. Summarize the heart of Peter's message.

2. When did Peter preach this message?

3. Does Peter cite Scripture in his preaching? If so, what does he cite?

4. What results came from the preaching of the Word?

5. Based on this outing, how would you characterize Peter as a testimony for Jesus? How would you rate his passion? His influence?

6. What can you learn from Peter's example that you can apply to your life?

When we read the book of Acts, we see the disciples literally on fire with the Gospel of Jesus Christ. Talk about holy passion! These men had spent serious time with Jesus and were recognized as having been with him. They preached and thousands converted. People followed them around in the hopes of being healed. We see them threatened yet remaining steadfast. They are models of the transformed life! But the very fact we are using the word "transformed" implies that they didn't start out the way that they ended up. Let's check out some of their early moments of following Jesus.

Read Matthew 14:22–33 and consider the following:

1. Who are the people on the boat? Where do they think Jesus is?

2. What was their emotional reaction when they saw the figure approaching? Why?

3. When Peter had the truth, how did he respond? What happened to his fear?

4. What circumstance caused the fear to return?

5. Based on the text, why do you think Peter started sinking?

6. What action did Peter take when the fear returned and he actually started going down?

7. What application can you make to your own life from what Peter experienced?

In walking on the water with Jesus and then sinking, Peter provides us with a highlight/lowlight moment all wrapped into one. Peter's all-time low, however, came with his firm attestation that he would stick with Jesus to the end and his subsequent three-time denial, complete with cursing, and general ugliness. We'll look at it as it appears in the gospel according to Luke.

Read Luke 22:31–34 and 22:54–61 and consider the following:

1. Have you ever had a Peter-type incident where you felt as though you totally blew it?
2. Consider the information with which Peter was armed. Did he know better than to deny Jesus? If so, does this have any application to you and me? (I don't know about you, but I have a tendency to beat myself up more over those sins where I knew better than to commit them.)
3. What have you learned from Peter's denial and subsequent restoration that you can apply in your daily walk?

While we could look further at the flaws of Peter, let's consider an early event in the life of John, who is often referred to as "the disciple whom Jesus loved."

Read Luke 9:51–56 and consider the following:

1. What is the situation in the passage that angers John and his brother?
2. How do they react?
3. What is Jesus' response?
4. What are we told that they all do at the end of verse fifty-six?
5. What did John and his brother learn from this experience?
6. What can we learn from John's ability to take a rebuke and move forward?

Peter and John messed up along the way, as we all do, but Jesus ignited in them a holy passion. They spent time with Jesus and were transformed! They heard the words of God and obeyed them. Neither was perfect, nor did they mature spiritually overnight, but God's Spirit indwelled them and changed them from scared and power hungry men into men of the Word who passionately and fearlessly carried the life-giving words of Jesus to a dying world! God did not let Peter and John stay the way they were when they first met Jesus. God loves us too much to let us remain the way we are!

Endnotes

1. For more information on Bible studies from Precept Ministries International, turn to the Bible Study Toolbox at the back of this book.

2. Kay Arthur, *How to Study Your Bible* (Eugene, Oregon: Harvest House, 1994).

3. Sandra Felton, *The Messies Manual* (Grand Rapids: Fleming H. Revell, 1984).

4. Richard J. Foster, *Celebration of Discipline* (San Francisco: Harper & Row, 1978).

5. Dallas Willard, *The Spirit of Disciplines* (New York: HarperCollins, 1988).

6. Dietrich Bonhoeffer, *The Cost of Discipleship* (New York: Touchstone, 1995).

Contact Information

If you'd like to invite Pam to speak to your group, you may contact her via e-mail at pamgillaspie@aol.com.

To sign up for Deep & Wide Bible reading reminders, go to www.deepandwide.org.

For more information on Precept Ministries International, write, call, or search the web at:

    Precept Ministries International
    P.O. Box 182218
    Chattanooga, TN 37422-7218
    1/800/763-8280
    www.precept.org